GAME
SET
LIFE

A Conversation on Character, Grit and the Power of Sports

by Jay Harris and Michael Kathrein

Copyright © 2025 by Jay Harris & Michael Kathrein

Cover & Layout Design: Mel Wise
Cover Photo: Katarina Dodig on Unsplash

Uploading or distributing photos, scans or any content from this book without prior permission is theft of the author's intellectual property. Please honor the author's work as you would your own. Thank you in advance for respecting the author's rights.

For permission requests, please contact the authors at:
HarrisTennisAcademy@yahoo.com

Game Set Life: A Conversation on Character, Grit and the Power of Sports

ISBN Paperback, 978-1-940498-41-6

ISBN Hardcover, 978-1-940498-44-7

ISBN eBook, 978-1-940498-45-4

I would like to offer some acknowledgement for the ability to complete this project. I must thank each and every one of my players. I would like to thank Chriss and John for their amazing guidance. Audrey, your support gives me the strength to complete the mission. Tim and Donna, your love always keeps me moving in the right direction. Thank you MaryJo, you always laugh at my antics. Matt, you're the best. Lainey, I love you and this is all for you. I am dedicating this book to my grandpa. He taught me the two most valuable lessons in life. He taught me to always put others first, and to make every day a rich full day. I think it is a good idea to thank my coauthor and brother, I guess, maybe. Ok, thank you. The people in this paragraph and the family that has stayed with me have made this project possible.

mk

Mom & Dad, you brought me into this world; thank you for not taking me out! But mostly, thank you for molding me into who I've become. To my sister and forever best friend, Nickie, you are a huge piece of this book about life; I cannot thank you enough Pips. And to my inner circle and favorite players, Jackson, Mason and Sharon, as our relationships continue to mature as we all age, I evolve as a person and absolutely love the effect you all have on me. I pledge to love you all always. For my life-long conversationalist, Michael, the process of writing this book with you became the sole purpose to finish. Thank you for your partnership. For my countless players, you have produced a platform that has allowed me to create a life's work. Your trust in me is appreciated more than any of you know.

jh

PREFACE

The first note from Jay:

As I sat in my sixth grade homeroom class, my first major "crush" sat two seats in front of me. Between the one and only Amy Gibson and I sat a boy named Mike. After creating a little courage (probably only *took* about six weeks), I asked Mike a simple question: can you ask Amy if she will "go with me"? In the 1980s, "going with" someone was synonymous with the act of becoming boyfriend/girlfriend. To my question, Mike quickly replied: "Of course I'll ask". A minute later (or less), Mike turned back to me and reported: "She said no, but that she still wants to be friends," and therein started a very interesting friendship between two very different kids where we would have thousands more back and forth "conversations" like that. Mike and I would later grow to become best friends, as Mike was one of the most loyal friends anyone could have. From defending me from "cool kids" who felt it was fun to pretend to be friends with me while actually working to make me look bad, to standing in as the best man at my wedding where he delivered a "powerful" speech about scratching, Mike has, for years, always been there and has endured a lot along the way!

In the spring of 1994 as I was transitioning out of a clinical psych graduate program as it was essentially exactly what I worried it might be (an educational battle as opposed to an educational endeavor), I found myself gravitating towards the fairly new field of Sports Psychology, and luckily, I was able to be admitted to what I would find out was an amazing Sports Studies Program at Miami University in Oxford, Ohio, just up the road from where my undergraduate studies ended at the University of Cincinnati.

In my first class at Miami, *Introduction to Sports Psychology*, while I was partaking in my first reading assignment, I was absolutely shocked to learn that some "psychologist" had "proven" in a study that sports do NOT build character. I literally had to read that line about six or seven times to make sure that I was reading it correctly, but yes indeed, I did read it right. Now, I was a boy who grew up in the most cliché of Midwest old school sporting households. My dad was a high school teacher who coached football, basketball and baseball (and later tennis!), and my mom was a former college athlete herself who competed in softball tournaments while pregnant with me and with me tagging around as a toddler, learning that apparently pooping in dugouts was not ok! SO, reading this truly had me puzzled. What I learned that day was a valuable piece of information and what I gained was an invaluable motivational life goal. First, I learned that in psychological research, the researcher can literally prove anything he/she wants by adjusting the variables and evaluation methods to skew the results in the favor of any theory that is trying to be "proven." Second, I gained an INTENSE motivation to disprove this study at every turn in my life. You see, in my own life, I felt that sports built about 95% of my character; so, how could this person say otherwise, let alone claim to prove otherwise? I was set to make sure anyone around me realized the importance and power of sports, and I was on my way to using sports as a tremendous vehicle for educational opportunities.

After struggling through the "what am I gonna be when I grow up" dilemma throughout graduate school, I sort of fell into a field that one could say was love at first sight. In the middle of a meeting my sister, Nickie, (a high school tennis star at the time) had with the new Miami head women's coach, I was offered a "hitter" position with the team, and that quickly morphed into an assistant coaching role. Looking back now, the dive into college coaching wasn't just a tremendous fit, but also provided me the path I had been looking for. As the son of a "movie kind of coach" maybe this path was a bit pre-destined for me. Or maybe I saw this as an opportunity to prove to my dad and my family that I wasn't "an embarrassment" (we will get into that story a bit later in this book)!

The first note from Mike:

If the sixth grade note passing situation happened today, I would upsell Jay to Amy more than I did back then. The kid sitting behind me was my competition for the girl and I'm not sure I put a good effort into it. I remember the sixth grade as the year I was sent to the emergency room twice. The quest for Amy wasn't the only thing we had in common. We both love to play, we play to win, and we had parents, family, teachers and coaches who were motivators. Some of them motivated us without them realizing the lifelong impact they would have on us.

Athletics have been a part of my life since I was a toddler. When I was born, my dad put a football in my crib. Whether it was football, baseball, or basketball, to me it was all the same. It was a chance to play. I grew up with stories of how great a basketball player my dad was in high school. There were many, many stories, and these stories were motivators. I loved to play, and so I was constantly seeking motivators. I found motivation in severe criticism, in a pat on the back, in a smile and nod of the head, in losing, in failure, and also in success. I cannot pick one motivator over another. Each played a vital role in developing me into a man, husband, dad, teacher, and coach.

A problem that is found in books about coaching, parenting, teaching, or athletics is that they are singular. Each book wants to pick one contributing factor for success and I find this to be untrue and limiting. I have yet to meet a singular person. People are complex and success is a process, not a singular action. I grew up playing the tier one sports of football, baseball and basketball. In school, I also added tennis and cross country to my athletic endeavors. I dabbled in many things but my love was basketball. It was the sport that I was most disadvantaged and had to work the hardest to just be on the team. I have coached tennis, baseball, basketball and golf. I have coached both girls' and boys' teams. The one constant in coaching has been golf, a sport I have coached for 28 years.

Jay and I have had many conversations about athletics and their importance to development. When he brought up the idea of writing a book about our experiences, I was excited. I started by asking Jay what he wanted to accomplish with the book. From that conversation, we gleaned that our ultimate goal is to help young athletes and parents, and maybe some coaches, understand the process of turning a love into success and maintaining that love for a lifetime.

I have taught over 3,500 students and coached over 1,000 athletes. That adds up to 9,000 parents. I want to share my experiences with student-athletes and the influence of parenting on the student-athlete. I have been very lucky to be around great kids and great parents. Some of the kids I coached were nice kids who played sports; some went to play college athletics at all divisional levels; and a few played professional sports, including former MLS, NFL, and NBA players. Each one of these students was unique but I have found some commonalities to the athletes' success.

Another note from Jay:

Well, it wouldn't be a true conversation if I didn't respond to Mike's verbiage, right? And THAT will be the "style" of writing used throughout this book actually. As Mike stated, we have had a lot of conversations about many things, but our most interesting ones in my opinion have been involving how experiences within the sports arena affect the personality and character development of kids. Our goal is to create a readable dialogue between us, replicating some of the conversations we have had, while also diving into some new areas we've both experienced, but have yet to truly discuss together.

I suppose that just in case Amy reads this book, I better mention some aspects of my resume as well! Soon after diving into the world of college coaching and experiencing two years as a graduate assistant for the 1996 MAC Champion Women's Tennis Program, I left Miami with a Master's Degree majoring in Sports Psychology and Sports Management, and became the youngest head coach of any Division I sport in the nation, as I accepted the head coaching position for the men at Bowling Green State University. At 24 years old (and looking closer to 18 at the time), some did not take me seriously; after using the rationale that my upward growth would far exceed that of the older candidates in the next five years with the hiring committee and having them buy into that and of course select me as their guy, I also became more confident in my ability to actually pull it off! I did have to push through my first set of goals (which included a sense to "not screw this team up too badly in the first year"). I then helped build a program that hadn't won a conference title in 36 years and turned it into a nationally ranked team and the 2000 & 2002 MAC Champions! After a punch in the gut (our tennis program was eliminated after the 2002 season), I was hired at Brown University as their head men's tennis coach. At Brown, I became the most successful coach in the 100-year history of their tennis program, as we won two Ivy League Titles, were ranked as high as 33 in the nation ("like 30"), earned the program's first two (and only) All-Americans advancing a doubles team to the NCAA Elite Eight, and developed two players who both later went on to advance to the quarterfinals of Wimbledon.

I did leave Brown in 2010 to enter the business world (kind of!) as I became a Director and General Manager at Sportime and the John McEnroe Tennis Academy. As a college coach, I had an incredible impact on my students, but after 16 years, I worked with just 47 players within my program. Joining the McEnroe Academy was going to give me an incredible opportunity to use my college experience to impact hundreds of kids every year. This was going to allow me to prove to an even greater degree that SPORT DOES BUILD CHARACTER and GRIT!

x

TABLE OF CONTENTS

PREFACE V

GRIT

LIFE IS ALL ABOUT STORIES. 3
LOVE THE STRESS. 23
CAN TOUGHNESS BE TAUGHT? 33
CONFIDENCE IS THE KEY. 53
BOOM MENTALITY. 65
FIRE VERSUS ANGER 75

POWER OF SPORTS

SETTING GOALS 85
LIFE CHOICES 93
QUITTING IS HABITUAL 105
MAKE YOUR LAST SHOT ALWAYS 123
THE NATURE OF THE
SPORT COMEBACK 129
POETRY OF SELF-TALK 135
A PICTURE IS WORTH
A THOUSAND WORDS 145
BEING A PERFORMER 155

CHARACTER

STOPLIGHT METHOD 165
THE MASTER TRANSLATORS. 177
MIDWEST MEETS THE EAST COAST 187
APPROACHING THE CHEATERS 197
YOU ALWAYS GOT MORE TO GIVE 207
THE ENTITLEMENT
MISSION STATEMENT 211
WHO DO YOU WANT TO BE
AS A FUTURE COLLEGE ATHLETE. 219
THE LAST SERVE 225
MEET THE AUTHORS. 227

PART ONE: GRIT

GRIT is often defined as the blend of passion and perseverance in a journey towards certain goals. Here in GAME SET LIFE, we agree, and as two super gritty kids who grew up with chips on our shoulders for various reasons, we wanted to use our stories to help our readers use GRIT to take them down a pathway of success and enhanced love for sports and maintain that love for life.

The grittiest players are often able to combine their intense work ethic and intelligent toughness with an ability to thrive within pressure situations and find learning opportunities after disappointing results. Where fear of loss or even embarrassment are present, these players CHOOSE to work harder to get themselves to believe that a difficult task at hand will be easy for them to accomplish. They can possess an unwavering focus that allows them to continuously enhance their level and pass by the seemingly more talented players. In addition to all of that, these athletes learn to truly control their own confidence allowing them to become more powerful on the field/court.

Great coaches are of course involved in building GRIT as they help players create amazing stories and navigate the balance between stoking the fire and showing players that they are supported and believed in. The ultimate goal is to have players leave the court/field after each session with more confidence than when they arrived.

We are confident that the juice will be worth the squeeze as you venture through this first section of GAME SET LIFE.

LIFE IS ALL ABOUT STORIES

A story has no beginning or end: arbitrarily one chooses that moment of experience from which to look back or from which to look ahead.

—Graham Greene

The butterfly effect is a very interesting concept. Can a butterfly flap its wings in western Africa and cause a hurricane in the Caribbean? A better question is can a person say hello to a stranger on the street and cause a tidal wave of positivity that affects millions of people? I believe the answer to the latter question is yes (I will leave the former to the scientists). It really is the foundation of civilization. It is the basic ideology of the major religions. The smallest of gestures can have a huge impact on not just the immediate person but for all those who come in contact with them.

Jay and I have different approaches to our stories. Jay would rush a stage at a One Direction concert just to get a photo to post on social media, and I like to acquire stories for myself privately.

Jay interrupts: ok maybe not One Direction—at least give me U2 or Guster!

Mike comes back: Jay may feel insulted by the One Direction stage rush but One Direction is far more recognizable than U2 or Guster right now. U2 is in the Hall of Fame; John Wayne is a Hollywood icon, and Jack Nicklaus is the greatest golfer of all time. However, very few people under 25 could identify any of them, but they sure as heck know One Direction.

I don't know how social media works, at least other than a few posts to Facebook. When I do something I do it just for myself. I stockpile my stories. I guess I have this vision of having grandchildren by my side spinning some of my memories for them. I might tell them any of my stories from my camping trips at many national parks, or the celebrities I have met (name dropping is a big part of storytelling), or I might tell the story of my great friend Matt.

I met Matt working at Galyan's Sporting Goods store in Columbus, Ohio. It was 1996, and I had just moved back to Columbus to get my teaching degree. I was working in the Fitness Department, selling thigh masters, treadmills, and stationary bikes to people trying to recapture their youth. And I loved it. By working there, I was able to get a good look at the struggles with fitness with a variety of people. But this story is about Matt.

Matt was in year seven of his college career, which started out as a basketball player at Wittenberg College. After a year that didn't work out, he transferred to Ohio State. Shortly after his transfer, Matt was diagnosed with testicular cancer; he had one testicle and several lymph nodes removed. Matt's cancer was all taken care of and things were good. We worked together for two years until I graduated. We were great friends and he was one of my groomsmen. He and I have many things in common but the glue of our friendship is our hatred for Sydney Crosby and the Penguins - just a light joke based on a ton of truth. Crosby may be a top citizen but we don't care.

A few years ago, Matt was once again diagnosed with testicular cancer. They were going to remove his other testicle. This time, Matt decided to have prosthetics implanted. This is the part of the story where things take an unexpected turn. On the morning of the surgery I was chatting with him while I was driving to the hospital. Of course, I was making many "ball" jokes. For example, he had spent 20 years with just one ball. How was he going to walk now that he was going to have two balls? I like to keep things light during most serious situations.

When I got to the hospital his mom was already in the room with him. The three of us were exchanging pleasantries when a nurse entered the room. She politely asked me to wait outside as she discussed matters with Matt. They talked for a few minutes and the nurse left the room. I walked back into the hospital room. Matt had a wry smile on his face so I asked him what was going on. The nurse told him that his surgery was going to be delayed a few hours because the hospital couldn't find his balls. I kid you not. The hospital lost his balls. Apparently, his prosthetic testicles were sent to the wrong hospital and someone had to drive to that hospital to get them.

Earlier I mentioned that Matt and I hate Crosby. I hate him because I am a Blue Jackets fan. Matt hates him because he is a Rangers fan. It was painful to type that. Matt was having a tough year and I knew he always wanted to see the Rangers play at Madison Square Garden. Fortunately, I know someone in New York. Jay was able to score tickets and a luxury box at the Garden, where they were playing the Ducks on December 23rd. Matt and I drove to New York that day. It took seven hours to get to New York and three hours to cross one bridge. Multiple times on the trip Matt mentioned how much he wanted to see the Christmas Tree at Rockefeller Center. The three of us went to dinner in the city and then went to the Garden. Matt was like a kid in a candy store. He had a constant look of amazement. When the game was over it was time to head to Rockefeller Center. We got there at 11:04pm. The tree was not lit up. Apparently, to save money, they turn the tree lights off at 11:00. Incredibly ironic because every other light in the city is left on 24 hours a day.

I did feel bad for Matt. He had a tough experience and he deserved to see the tree in all its glory. He survived cancer twice, the hospital lost his balls and all he wanted was some lights. Matt spent the next hour complaining but a few cocktails straightened him up. All three of us drove back to Ohio the following morning. Jay is a good old boy from Ohio who had to get home for Christmas. When we got back to Mansfield, we dropped Jay off at his parents' house. Matt dropped me off at home and then he went back to Columbus. We each had a nice Christmas Eve and Christmas day with our families.

The day after Christmas, Jay's family and my family were playing our annual "kids vs adults" basketball game at our high school. After Cole had changed the rules for the tenth time, it was time to take a break. I checked my phone and I had a missed call from Matt. I gave him a quick call back to see how his Christmas went. When Matt answered the phone I naturally asked how he was doing. I was not expecting his response. Matt said he had a heart attack and was in the hospital. Seriously, this guy had a terrible year — cancer, for the second time, lost balls, unlighted Christmas tree, and now a heart attack.

Life is all about stories, but where the story begins and then travels to is completely up to the story-teller. Matt's story could have focused on all the great moments in his life or completely on the hardships, but my focus was on all of those moments meshed. People learn more from their mistakes than their successes and athletes learn more from their failures than their wins. People learn history so they don't repeat it (at least they shouldn't). But it is so very important to tell the whole story.

> **Jay chiming back in:** Mike, that's an awesome story and you are right, Matt is a great guy. You did forget to add that I apologized for allowing New York to almost kill Matt! What a year the poor guy had, but he did have an incredible trip (sans a few lights). And that is where I'll begin my thoughts on the topic of Life being about stories.
>
> First, I'll have to disagree slightly with Mike's view of my approach to stories. While I would for sure rush to a stage and stand with Bono to hang out, and I would for sure take some pics and post them on social media and text them to many friends, the goal of putting myself in position to create an incredible story is really to EXPERIENCE the story myself, and then the sharing of the story to others has a dual benefit. First, it allows the listener/

reader/social media viewer of the story the benefit of envisioning that amazing experience, and second, it allows me personally to re-experience that event every time I get to tell the story! As I recently said to my oldest son, Jackson, sometimes you just have to squeeze in as much life as you can.

The saying "Life is about Stories" for me came from one of my college coaching mentors, Jeff Zinn. Coach Zinn played tennis at the University of Cincinnati about 10 years before I was a player there in the early 90s. Jeff had grown up in the Queen City and after graduating from UC, went on to a very successful college coaching career. I first met Jeff when we were set to room together at one of the top recruiting camps in the country down in Florida, the Ed Krass College Tennis Academy. I was a young head coach at Bowling Green State University and Jeff was the head coach for a top 20 program at Wake Forest. I was excited to meet my fellow Bearcat and as I walked into the hotel room, he immediately yelled out a big hello. The hello came from the bathroom and as I walked up to the open bathroom door to say hello back, I looked in and let's just say that I saw everything I needed to see. That was the first of many stories Coach and I would "create," and towards the end of that week after we had some great experiences together, Coach Zinn gave me some great advice. He said "Life is all about stories," and as simple as that statement may have seemed, it became immortalized in my head. I learned, in that moment, to embrace and appreciate ALL of the experiences that I would be lucky enough to have, and not only did I immediately change my personal mindset when it came to "seizing the day" (or following Robin William's advice in The Dead Poet's Society which was "carpe diem"), but I also set out to share that mindset with any of the players I coached and especially those I became close to.

One of my favorite players I have ever coached, Danny Pellerito, certainly has learned to grasp the idea of embracing the opportunities to create and experience stories. One of the first stories that Danny and I created together actually involved Mike! Danny was a very talented 11-year old tennis player, and was on the cusp of being nationally ranked, but had a hard time controlling his emotions. There were days that he would just burst into tears during practice! That's right Allen Iverson, I said PRACTICE! I was asked to be one of Danny's coaches, and initially, my biggest coaching role was to work with Danny on emotional control and on creating some skills to build his self-confidence. Danny was already one of my favorite kids. He was extremely passionate and also had a great sense of humor. One day while coaching a group with a focus on hitting balls with court depth, I yelled out to a player: "that has to be deeper." Danny was standing next to me and quickly replied: "That's what she said. He was 11!! Some coaches may have been appalled by that. I simply thought: this guy is going to be the best college teammate ever! Anyway, one afternoon, Danny and I were in one of our off-court sessions, and Danny started telling me a story about prank-calling his friends. He then asked if he could prank call one of my friends. I told him that if he focused during our session, he could do it at the end. That may have been our best session ever; he was so focused! I'm a man of my word, so at the end, I allowed him to prank call one of my friends. At this point, you can of course guess who that was. Now, I won't go into details about the criteria of this particular call as I don't want to incriminate Danny, but let's just say that Danny had to hang up quickly after Mike threatened to call the police on him, and a minute later Mike called my cell to tell me about this call he had just gotten from a kid claiming to be his son! Oh wait, did I incriminate Danny there? Whoops!

Mike interrupts: Jay, you didn't rush the stage for Bono. You rushed it for Milli Vanilli.

Jay responds: But it wasn't them singing!

Mike continues: Interesting point about creating the story for sharing and learning purposes. If that is what you are doing it for, then I am glad you got Milli Vanilli's autograph. Do you think the song *Girl You Know It's True* has a teaching point? I tease Jay because he has done some really stupid things in the name of getting the photo op, but he has done some interesting and valuable things too. The first school superintendent that I worked for at Highland Local Schools gave me some great advice that speaks to what Jay is trying to convey.

The first day of a school year all the teachers and staff get together for a meeting. Typically, the superintendent addresses the troops, and in this year, a very short and simple story was told. He told us about a day when he was forced to substitute teach in class, and the teacher didn't have a lesson plan for him to follow. It was a subject that he hadn't taught and didn't know enough to even fake it. So, he improvised. He reached into his pocket and pulled out the contents. He then explained what each item was and somehow connected those to stories about himself. I heard that speech 28 years ago and I still think very highly of his advice about the importance for teachers to truly connect with their students. Kids like stories, and they like to relate to teachers/coaches. While I may not be a social media poster as Jay knows, the memories that I log daily become fodder for stories that help me connect to countless students and athletes, and this in return, provides a path for me as a teacher and coach to build great relationships with my students and players.

> **Jay interrupts:** Well that's because you have a photographic memory! During one of our first great conversations we had about the book, I stopped and said "Shoot, we should have recorded this!" You replied: "I'll remember." It was like when Jimmy Chitwood said "I'll make it."

Back to Mike's voice: I don't blindly post my memories for the world. I share my memories with people when the time is appropriate. For example, I was trying to give a pep talk to my team about being there for your friends and teammates. Whenever I do things like this I try to give an example of being a good teammate and being a bad teammate, being a good friend and being a bad friend.

I told my team an unusual story about a trip to St. Thomas. It was a great vacation with three of my friends, and Jay was one of them. The four of us decided to take the ferry to St. Johns for the day to check out this great beach they had on the island. The beach (Trunk Bay) absolutely lived up to the hype. This particular beach had an underwater reef that snorkelers could explore. All four of us got our snorkeling gear on and headed out to do some exploring. It was amazing. I would just drift along the top of the water reading the signs attached to the reef. Every once in a while the water would get deep but then I would come to a sandbar for a rest. Eventually the signs stopped but the wildlife was fun to encounter so I just kept drifting along. Then, I realized that I was alone. I pulled my head out of the water and I couldn't see anyone or land. I had drifted too far out and the waves made it so I could not see which way the beach was. I was so panicked at this point. I had to make a guess on which way to swim. I decided that the current forced me to drift this way so I needed to swim against the current to get back to safety. I swam so fast I could have beaten Michael Phelps. Of course, I was wearing flippers, but come on, I would need some advantage to beat him!

After what seemed like an eternity, I could see the beach and safety. Absolutely exhausted I climbed out of the water and found Jay and the others. Extremely pissed off I then yelled at them for leaving me. Seriously, was it too much to ask for them to tap me on the shoulder and say they were turning back. I then did the only reasonable thing. I stomped off to the cabana bar to pout about my terrible friends. While sitting at the bar I started talking to a girl. Again, I lost track of time and my friends.

At the beginning of the day we made a plan to catch the five o'clock ferry back to St. Thomas because we were going to a restaurant on the other side of the island. When I realized that it was already five o'clock I rushed over to my friends spot on the beach to find that they had left. Did they really ditch me again? I quickly gathered my stuff and headed to the marina to catch that ferry. I was too late, and I had to wait for the next ferry, which was in a little over an hour. Right next to the ticket window for the ferry was an ice cream shop. I walked into the shop and ordered a strawberry cheesecake ice cream with a waffle cone. To this day it is the best ice cream I have ever had. I took to the cone outside and sat on the dock with my feet just dangling over the water. I slowly enjoyed the ice cream, savoring every bite. The ice cream had bits of cinnamon pie crust in it. With each bite I watched all of the comings and goings. From time to time a person on a boat would wave to me as if we were old acquaintances. I tell this story for two reasons. One reason is to show that sometimes good friends will treat you badly. It doesn't make them bad, it just makes them human. The second reason is how the day turned out. I could have been killed at sea but I wasn't. Instead I got to talk to a pretty girl and enjoy a great ice cream cone. Perspective changes the story.

> **Jay's turn on the stand:** WOW, I know I'm getting old, and I realize that was almost 30 years ago, but how do I not remember that you were abandoned? Ok, I'm on the stand here, so I have to be careful not to incriminate myself, right? (an east coast fear - covered in a later chapter!). Well, I am truly an Ohio boy, and because of that, I have no problem saying that I AM SORRY WE ABANDONED YOU!! I also realize that wasn't the only time, so sorry about that too!! I'm happy about the pretty girl though, and also was happy about the pretty girl (Celine) that I met there, but being from New York now, I'll be careful not to incriminate myself with that story! Ha
>
> Mike and I both LOVE stories. We love to tell them and we love to listen to them. I'm currently writing another book of comical short stories, which is a compilation of ridiculous experiences I've had during my college playing and coaching days. It looks like I'm going to have to ask Mike to write a chapter in that one!

This book is a little different though. We want the reader to get to know us a bit through certain stories we will tell, and while we hope those will garner a laugh or two, that isn't the purpose. Our goal is to allow the reader to understand the perspective we have so that they will better understand what we are attempting to give them. We would like the reader to feel our passion for sports, to live certain experiences from our point of view, and to (as Mike said) learn how to turn a love into success and maintain that love for a lifetime.

Back to Mike: I always find the perspectives that people take from a story or encounter fascinating. I don't know how many times that I have been talking with a person and said to myself "wow, that was their takeaway from that conversation?" When I am telling a story I have a specific goal that I want to reach. The story is very clear in my head but somehow the story comes out of my mouth differently or reaches my listener's ears differently. As a coach, I love to share stories because I think they are teaching a lesson. However, I can't always be certain my athlete is getting the correct takeaway.

So, I try to keep the stories short, be direct, and then follow up with questions to see if they understood the point I was trying to make. Stories of my past mistakes could help prevent misfortunes for my students/players. After 28 years of coaching I have acquired a great deal of stories but I found that I am talking less and less. When instructing, I want the player to get many reps in and gabbing too much could be hindering. Players need to acquire their own stories, and this is done by playing and getting in reps. I don't want my athlete's story to be "I had this coach who never stopped talking."

Jay adds: So many tennis coaches are known for over-talking or over-coaching. I guess those are two different things with over-talking being worse than over-coaching. At least with over-coaching there's intent to be a good coach and to be helpful, whereas with over-talking that's used as a filler of time because the coach doesn't truly believe that he/she has something valuable to give the student. While it's important to create a relationship with the student, and sometimes telling stories is a great way to do that, as Mike referred to, over-talking is simply a coaching mistake.

Mike is back: I recently had a morbid conversation with my family. I didn't think it was morbid but they did. I was talking to my daughter about why she was so afraid of so many things. She insisted that she wasn't afraid, but she is afraid. Lainey is hesitant to do anything dangerous because she is afraid of getting hurt or dying. As a dad, I guess I like her approach to safety. As a mentor, I object. Here is the morbid part of the story. I often sleep with my house door unlocked. My family hates this but I live in a great area where people do this. But more importantly to the story, I told her I don't think about people breaking into the house and hurting me because I am not afraid of dying. I have done so much; I have seen so much; and I have experienced so much; that if I die tomorrow I know I had a rich, full life. Please don't be mistaken. I am not looking to go anywhere any time soon. The point I am making is that I want players to get the most out of every day.

One of my favorite stories is about the bank of 86,400. If a player woke up and found $86,400 in their bank account what would they do? The money comes with a caveat though. The player isn't allowed to save any of the money. They have to use every last penny of it. The following day another $86,400 will be deposited in their account with the same caveat, and this will happen every day of their life. But they can't bank any of the money, ever. Consider it a fire sale, everything must go. Well, every day each person is given 86,400 seconds to make use of. Nobody can bank any of the time. All of the time must be spent. The big question is how is a player going to spend that time? Are they going to sleep for 43,200 seconds? Are they going to check social media for 10,800 seconds? Are they going to play games on their phone or Xbox for 10,800 seconds? This particular player has already used 64,800 seconds and they haven't even had anything to eat yet. In addition, what stories will the player have to tell? If a player is going to have a rich full day they have to sleep a little less and play on their phones a little less.

One of the keys to success in athletics for an athlete is knowing what they want from that particular sport. Once a player knows what they want they can start developing their story. I like to think of every endeavor as a story. I also always try to view the story as the reader, not the narrator. When I am involved with a project I want to know how others are viewing me. I know what I want people to think, but is that what they are actually seeing? The reason this is important is that most people have a certain amount of vanity. By vanity I mean people want to be liked and respected. If a person can see themselves from a different perspective, it can motivate them to be better. Sometimes it is difficult to see the other perspective.

One day not very long ago I was chatting with the cart guy at the golf course. I was on pro shop detail this particular day and Brad was working the carts. I looked out of the window and saw Brad sitting in a cart with his feet up on the dash and he was talking on the phone. So, I walked out to him to see what was going on because there were four or five dirty carts that needed to be cleaned and put away. I asked him if everything was going well and he then laid into a rant about how the previous cart guy doesn't do his job. Brad ranted about trash being left in carts, gas tanks half empty, and they weren't put away properly. As I looked around I saw several of the same issues on his shift. So, I asked him "how is that different from what you are doing right now?"

I have heard countless numbers of players complain about their teammates. I remember this one golfer who talked about how much better they were than the player playing the spot ahead of him. He ranted about how much farther he hit the ball and his immaculate short game. I listened to him until he was all ranted out and then I asked him, "Then why are his scores lower than yours?" About 20 years ago I was an assistant baseball coach. One evening I got a phone call from an angry parent. His son was a junior playing predominantly on the JV team but did get a little varsity time. This particular parent thought his son was the greatest second baseman in years at Lexington High School. I listened to the parent rant until he was all ranted out, and then I asked him what exactly he wanted. He didn't think his son was getting a fair chance at the varsity level. He only played an inning or two and got an occasional at-bat. The parent wanted his son to start the next conference game and then I would see his skillset. Well I wasn't about to start him. Not because the parent asked me to but rather because I didn't want him to fail. The next game he played in was a JV game; where he had two errors in the field including an easy pop fly and went zero for four at the plate. He did get several foul tips though.

Jay quips: Just foul tips, nice! Sorry, I couldn't resist!

Mike continues: Parents and coaches have a small but important role in developing a player's story. The primary character in the story should be the player with everyone else serving as the supporting cast. A coach's job is to support their players. Pre and post-season meetings have been a key component towards this support for me as a coach. In these sessions, I don't take notes; I just sit and listen. When the player has finished, I ask them "what can I do to help?" so the player will know that I am a supporting member in their story. Now, this isn't a situation where the inmates rule the asylum. I establish the rules and expectations of the members of the golf program and these are clearly defined and actually confirmed with a signed contract. However, I want the players to be invested in the program and allowing them to write their own stories within the parameters of the program builds their investment. I have never told a player what their goals were. A player must develop their own goals and the coach then needs to do all they can to help the player achieve those goals.

If a player wants to play golf at the collegiate level, I will lay out a plan to accomplish this goal. I start by asking a series of questions to find out exactly what type of collegiate experience the player is looking for. For example, what level do they want to play? Playing

Division One golf has a more challenging path than Division Two or Three. Do they want to go to a competitive program? Do they want to stay close to home? The list of questions goes on and on. Typically, the player's eyes get a little glossy and they get overwhelmed because they had no idea so many decisions needed to be made. These questions start to focus the player. It will force them to narrow their goals and show them how much they have to work to accomplish the goals.

A parent must play a similar role as the coach. I believe that most coaches know their roles in a player's story but I am not sure most parents know their role. Too many parents want to write the player's story. It is important for a parent to be involved with their child but there is a fine line between involved and controlling. Some parents see their children as an extension of themselves. The parent tries to relive their own childhood through their children. Almost everyone would like a second shot at high school. Call it a shot at redemption. They think they can correct all of the mistakes they made growing up by forcing their children to be perfect. This is a huge mistake. The mistakes are the things we learn and grow from. Parents have to let children make mistakes. They should just be careful to not to allow too big of a mistake and to be there to catch the child when they fall. A parent needs to be a supporting cast member, but not the narrator of the story.

It is very difficult to see oneself as they truly are. That is why it is important to try to see oneself from another person's point of view. When an athlete does this successfully they know what they need to do to improve. If a person wants to play number one on a golf team they know exactly what that will take. They have the ability to see who is the number one player and what scores they need to shoot to take that spot. The player then can practice harder, longer, and smarter to write their story. I have a player right now that has worked incredibly hard but wasn't getting the results she wanted. As soon as the season was over she began to rewrite her story. She began driving to Columbus, Ohio (an hour away) four days a week to get better. Her parents enrolled her in a program designed to help get high school golfers into major Division I programs, but her focus wasn't college, it was simply to improve. So, she began rewriting her story. As her coach I have asked her about her progress.

I asked her what she was working on, did she like the program, and what could I do to help. I would listen to her answers and invite her to tell me stories. The program she was involved with included swing coaches, physical trainers, sports psychology, and college recruitment. She would tell me stories about each of these facets within the program. Her stories were beneficial for two reasons. It helped her reflect on her own progress, and it gave me more coaching tools to use for other players. I am always looking to improve and any little story that I am told can make me better. The greatest benefit is that it makes my player the hero of her own story, and this is a must.

Telling stories is very important in coaching, but a coach must be careful in storytelling because a coach never really knows what is being heard. I had this player, Sarah, and I was close with her family. Sarah and her dad and my daughter and I played many rounds of golf together. We even went on vacation together. So, I had a different relationship with her than other players. I felt I could talk to Sarah differently than other players. Since I knew more about her than other players our conversations could be more personal. I talked to her more in a father and daughter manner rather than just as a player and coach.

One day about mid-summer I noticed that Sarah wasn't really engaging with her teammates. Soon after that, she wasn't making eye contact with me and was starting to really isolate herself. So, I gave her dad a call and asked "what's up with Sarah?" He said nothing, she was fine. I explained what I was observing and he said she is just quiet. I wasn't buying it. Whenever a player has a prolonged change in behavior something is going on. Sarah had put a lot of work into her game and I wanted her to have success and fun with the upcoming season. However, as the weeks went on leading up to the start of the season Sarah was still isolated. The season started and on the first trip Sarah stared out of the window for the two hours to the golf course.

When the players went to the practice range to warm-up I called her dad and told him about her behavior. He told me to pull her aside and talk to her. So I did.

Sarah told me that nothing is wrong and that all is well. I wasn't buying it. The team and Sarah had a good tournament and players were happy, except for Sarah. She once again stared out of the window all the way home. The next day I pulled Sarah aside after practice and asked her what was going on. She repeated herself and said nothing was wrong. I told her that I was gearing the season toward her. I wanted her to have success because of all her hard work and most importantly, I wanted her to have fun. I pointed out that her behavior toward me and the team had changed and that typically indicates that there is an issue. I told her that if I had done something to offend or upset her that I wanted to know about it. If Sarah didn't tell me what I had done, then I was likely to continue to upset her. I gave some examples of the change in behavior and reiterated that I wanted to help her. During the conversation I repeated many times that I wanted her to have fun and would do whatever it took to make that happen.

As a father of a daughter I would be ecstatic if a coach or teacher said something like that to my daughter. Here is an adult telling a kid that they will do whatever it takes to help the kid have fun and a great season. This was not Sarah's takeaway. To this moment I have no idea what she heard in that conversation or what she told her parents. Within an hour I got an angry text from her dad stating "I was doing all I could to get Sarah to quit." There were many angrier words in the text. I immediately gave him a call, but he didn't answer. I sent him a text saying that a conversation is in order after a text like that. He came back with a few more angry texts and then blocked me. I had a million thoughts running through my head. Mainly, it was "what in the world did I do or say to cause that reaction?"

After a couple of days and some social media shaming (by Sarah's mom), her dad unblocked me and we met to discuss the texts. I told him my intention with the conversation and what I said to her. I don't think he believed me though. Worse, Sarah's behavior became more disrespectful. She ignored me and some team rules. I turned the other cheek because I was very disappointed and confused. I hated where things were and the direction things were headed with Sarah and her family. I gave her dad another call, and said the three of us need to sit down and get this figured out or the season would be wasted. He agreed and we decided to meet at my house. I wanted to hit a homerun with this meeting. I wanted Sarah back fully engaged with the team and having fun. Sarah's family loves Greek food. So, I drove to Columbus (60 miles each way from Lexington) to get all of their favorite things to eat. I got their favorite drinks and set the meeting time to correspond with a soccer game I knew they would enjoy. I was ready to win this player back. About an hour before they were set to arrive at my house I got a phone call from them. They weren't coming. They never did come over and we never met to figure things out. Today, I still don't know what Sarah's takeaway was.

Sarah's story is quite tragic but there was something that I learned. I still try to engage with players and I still tell my stories. However, now I constantly ask questions during my conversations. I do this to make sure the player is getting the correct takeaway. I highly recommend doing this for coaches and parents. Kids are highly impressionable. Adults need to make sure they are making positive impressions. Parents and coaches know what they want to say to players but what the player is hearing is uncertain. Asking questions throughout the conversation can clear up any misconceptions. I know I failed with Sarah and her family, and that is the tragedy. I miss them.

> **Jay brings this first chapter to a close:** As much as I of course agree with Mike stressing the importance of avoiding his students having misconceptions, I will admit using a rather sneaky coaching method that actually has the opposite intentions. Using this method could produce disastrous results unless used carefully, at the right time, and with a student who trusts the coach wholeheartedly! Here is a story that demonstrates this:

In the spring of 2004, my Brown Bears tennis team was ranked in the top 40 of all Division I tennis programs in the country. Our number one doubles team was ranked #7 in the country, and we had two other players ranked in the country as well. Anyone ever associated with Ivy league tennis knows that April is the most important month of the year. That is when all Ivy matches are played, when the Ivy League Champion is crowned, and then when qualifiers head to the NCAA Tournament. That April, we began our quest to win the Ivies with a match in Philadelphia against the University of Pennsylvania. We were heavy favorites, but as with any opener, the unknown is a little scary. The fear factor was real during the opening doubles point (a college tennis match starts with three doubles matches, and the team that wins two of the three matches wins the "doubles point" and goes up 1-0 in the race to four points). The Brown Bears came out so tight that even our #1 doubles team (two guys ranked #7 in the country who both later in their tennis careers advanced to the quarterfinals of Wimbledon!) found themselves in a deep hole. Somehow, we held on to win the doubles point, but we were rattled. Going into the singles matches (six of them worth one point apiece) five of our six guys carried the tension right back onto the court. However, our lone freshman, Cincinnati native, Eric Thomas, went on the court playing #4 singles and apparently didn't know any better than to fear being nervous, and he went out and won 6-0, 6-0 in his Ivy match opener. It was truly an impressive performance and put us up 2-0. Much work was to be done though as the rest of the boys were all struggling. My toughest competitor, Ben Brier, a senior captain on the team, was struggling the most. Ben was playing #5 singles and when Eric walked off his court, Ben had just lost the first set of his match 7-6 and then had his serve broken to start the second set. That is when I walked onto the court to have a little chat with Ben.

Walking onto the court, I could obviously see how hard Ben was fighting, but also how hard he was fighting his own demons.

I decided to take a little bit of a risky approach, but one that I was confident would push the right buttons. I came up to Ben and calmly and quietly said this: "Ben, for so long, you have been our toughest guy. I really thought so. But today, I am just wondering if I was wrong. I mean, our freshman over there just walked on the court playing #4; you are playing #5; he was playing #4 and he went out and won 0 & 0, and you, Ben, just lost a set to this guy? I don't know man. I don't know." And then I turned and walked away shaking my head (for extra effect!). I knew Ben would be mad. But I also knew he was a fighter. I figured that if I could get him to fight ME a bit, fight against what I said to him, that he would stop focusing on how bad HE was playing. Ben won the next two sets 6-2, 6-1 and was the guy who ended up clinching the team win for us. That's not the best part of the story though!

After the match, Ben stormed up to me and said:

"Coach, I am so mad at you right now! I can't believe what you said to me out there!! I can't believe that you would question my toughness like that!!"

I then calmly asked: "Ben, can I ask you a question?"

Ben said: "yes, what?"

I said: "Ben, what was the score when I walked onto the court?"

Ben said: "I lost the first and was down 1-0 in the second!"

I said: "And what happened after I left?"

Ben exclaimed: "What?!!"

I then raised my voice and said: "WHAT HAPPENED AFTER I LEFT?!"

Ben thought for a moment and then said: "Wait, you did that on purpose?"

I exclaimed: "BEN, WHAT IS MY JOB HERE?! OF COURSE I DID THAT ON PURPOSE!!"

Ben then said: "Shit, you Mr. Miyagi'd me!"

Now, many could say that my approach here was VERY risky and could have resulted in a much different result and maybe could have even damaged my relationship with my player. But that is the thing; I knew that wasn't possible. I knew Ben. I knew him so well that I KNEW how he would respond. And if he didn't respond the way that I expected him to (with toughness), then I knew how disappointed he would be in himself and even THAT would push him to improve. In a strange way, it was a win/win. The key of course is for a coach to truly know his player, and if a coach knows his player to this level, then I believe that coach is then able to create some AMAZING STORIES!

LOVE THE STRESS

Toughness equals the ability to get yourself to believe that a difficult task at hand will be easy for you to accomplish.

— *Jay Harris*

One of the first super important lessons I learned in my studies in the Miami University Sport Psychology program was this concept of "loving stress." It is sort of a strange concept to most, as society has so often painted stress to be the bad guy. Stress is the thing to avoid, the thing to control, the thing to fear. But what I learned was to take a completely different perspective when it comes to stress, and the power one can create if able to do so.

In the finals of the 2022 Australian Open tennis championship, Rafael Nadal was on the verge of creating history once again, as he stood one match away from winning a record 21st grand slam tournament. However, at the age of 34 he was matched against the hottest of young players, Daniil Medvedev, and his chances were not great to take the title. He then lost the first two sets and also found himself down 2-3, love-40 in the third, essentially one point away from his chance being taken away. Then it happened. Nadal LOVED that moment. Nadal loved the situation he was in! Somehow, he loved that he was down two sets to love, against this incredible player, and seemingly insurmountable odds. He somehow won that game to even the third set score at 3-3. Then he won that set 6-4. Then he dug deep enough to win the fourth set 6-4 putting himself just a set away from this historic title. In the face of that "pressure," after fighting all the way back and putting himself in a situation to win the match, overcoming these insurmountable odds, Nadal faltered a bit. Nadal found himself up 5-4 serving in the fifth, just a couple points away from winning the 21st title, but Medvedev broke him. Five-all. I'm going to go out on a limb to say that about 99.5% of the players possibly of all time on the professional tour would've then lost those next two games to give away that title. But not Nadal. Nadal simply loved that moment. He broke Medvedev right back to go up 6-5, and then held his serve the next game at love, to capture his 21st grand slam title, putting him atop the Mount Rushmore of tennis. Nadal loves the stress. Renowned coach, Patrick Mouratoglou (of course Michael would say: "Patrick who?") stated after the match as he gave his insight on how Nadal somehow won: he said Nadal's number one quality is his resilience and love for the situations where he faces the toughest moments. It makes him feel alive. Other players don't like when it's tough. Nadal loves it.

Mike responds: You are right, Jay, I don't know Patrick Mouratoglou. That doesn't mean he isn't renowned. I just don't have time to follow tennis. The last time I was following tennis Monica Seles and Pete Sampras were dominating, and John McEnroe was playing in a band. I do think I might need some therapy though because I love the stress. Many coaches and influential sports figures refer to loving the stress as "don't be afraid of the moment." However, because the brain often doesn't comprehend the negative word and will only hear "be afraid," I love Jay's positive spin to get the message across better.

Personally, I have always loved the stress. The stress challenges me. The stress forces me to be better. The stress gives me an adrenaline boost. This is not to say that I always succeed and conquer the stress. It just means I love the challenges stress creates. When I was finishing up my Master's degree I had two options. I could write a thesis or complete a Capstone project. A few years later degree candidates were given a third option. They were able to take a comprehensive exam in lieu of the writing projects. The writing projects were completed over a period of time and under the supervision of an advisor. The exam was completed in four hours and was completed without any assistance. Most degree candidates were still choosing the writing options and had no interest in the exam. I would have chosen the exam. The exam would be stressful for sure, but why not? The exam forces me to prepare, to study, and to improve myself. It also is a challenge. I always look at exams as a personal contest between myself and the professor. There is no way I will let a professor beat me.

I have heard the phrase "pressure is a privilege" or an equivalent phrase many times, but what is meant by the phrase and how does pressure make a player a better performer? To answer the question, it is best to know where pressure comes from. There is a debate out there on whether pressure is self-induced. A player creates the pressure in his or her own mind. Let's say a basketball player gets fouled going in for a game winning layup with just one second left on the clock. When the player goes to the free throw line, most people will make the assumption that there is a lot of pressure on the player to make the free throw so the team can win the game. How is the free throw with one second left any different than a free throw in the first quarter? Each free throw is worth the same amount of points. Why is so much value added to the free throw with one second left? If the player misses the free throw with one second left and the team loses the game, will other players on the team think about the free throws they missed throughout the game? Or, will they simply blame the player who missed last one for the loss? I recently played a really good round of golf setting my personal record as well as a course record. I told Jay about the round and he was impressed with the score. A few days later I was talking to Jay and I told him I was on my way to the golf course. Jay said, "I can't believe you are playing golf again after your last round!" This is a very interesting statement. The last hole on the golf course I was playing is a par 5. I was on the green in two and had an eight-foot putt for eagle. I missed the eagle putt but still made a birdie. If I would have made the eagle putt, then I would have had three eagles in a round and shot a rare score. Not once did I fester about missing that putt. Instead I thought of the par I made on hole 16, which is a great birdie opportunity. In basketball every missed shot matters, no matter when the miss occurs. In golf every missed opportunity matters, not just on hole 18.

Of course I understand that in basketball you have fans cheering and their days are made or lost depending on whether their players make the winning shot. I understand that no one wants to be viewed as the player who missed the free throw to lose a game. However, players need to play with a sense of urgency from the very beginning of a competition. Playing with a sense of urgency will help avoid the pressure situations late in competitions. I don't really believe pressure is completely self-induced. Fans, coaches, parents and teammates all contribute to creating pressure. So, let me address why pressure is a privilege. If we go back to the basketball game, think about how many players are sitting on the bench watching the game. They didn't give themselves the opportunity to play under the pressure. In golf, how many players have a chance to make an eight-foot putt on the 72nd hole to win the U.S. Open?

> **Jay's turn:** Lots of great questions there, Mike! I'm hoping the reader is thinking a bit. I want to address a few of them.
>
> The first is to answer the question, why is the free throw with a second left in a game different from the others? Fear is the answer. We all have fear inside us. Some feel it more than others. Some who may feel it a lot can control it well. People also fear different things of course! If I'm at the free throw line at the end of my UHoops basketball game (as I recently was in our National Tournament in NYC), many unproductive thoughts flood my brain! Ugh. I would of course have the fear that if I miss, we are going to lose. I would fear letting my teammates down. I would fear my own personal judgment of my own mental strength and toughness if I wasn't able to find a way to make the shot. I may fear the embarrassment of others thinking that I choked. Now, I can't control the initial onslaught of those thoughts, BUT, I can control how my brain responds to them! For example, in that

National Tournament in NYC, as Terrell Suggs (former enemy of the Cleveland Browns when he played for the Ravens) watched and scouted our team, I had all of the fears that I just mentioned. So what did I do? Well, the first thing is that I know myself well. I knew they were coming, so I wasn't surprised, and that made it pretty easy to shield them away. Next, I knew I had to REPLACE the "thought chamber" in my head with a new, positive thought. So, I looked at my teammates on the bench and visualized them getting excited when I made that free throw. Then, I FOCUSED on the task at hand. I've taken lots of these shots; I went to my trusted routine; I repeated my reminder line (further explanation in the self-talk chapter) "stay tall," and then I swished that free throw pointing to my teammates on the bench right after sort of thanking them for the first positive thought.

I love almost all sports. I really love basketball, but I also really love tennis (while hating it at times too). At 51 years old, I made a bit of a tennis comeback this summer (2023). I hadn't played a competitive tennis match in five years and hadn't played a tournament in eight. One may ask why. Well, tennis is my career and when I have a racquet in my hand almost every day, sometimes adding more court time isn't the preferred way to spend time. Nonetheless, I chose to go back and compete in my hometown tournament, the Mansfield News Journal. My first EVER tournament win was at the NJ in 1983 as I took down Doug Hartzler 6-4, 6-0 in the finals to avenge a loss earlier that summer to Doug in the finals of my first tournament ever, the Miss Ohio (I did get a kiss on the cheek from Miss Ohio at the trophy presentation for being runner-up though, which was my real motivation to play that tournament!). The NJ always had a special place in my heart as I played every year from '83 to '94 and then some scattered years after that after becoming a full-time coach and living mostly on the east coast. I've won over 30 NJ titles in various divisions and while I DO realize this is just a small hometown tournament, I do feel the need to preserve the little "legacy" there when choosing to go back. Because of that "pressure," I get nervous when playing. This year, the nerves were compounded a bit by the fact that I really had no idea what level I would be able to play. I AM getting older, so the unknown was a little scary.

I went into my first singles match as a heavy favorite, but found myself playing really bad and went down 4-1 in the first set. I actually asked myself: "am I really this bad now?" I was too competitive to believe the answer was yes, so I replaced all of the negative thoughts and fears with an intense desire to solve a puzzle. How could I get my old body and fuzzy brain to perform at a level good enough to win this match? The first step was to love being where I was. I had to love the stress, especially because I was the one creating it! So that's what I did. I loved the puzzle that was in front of me and the challenge that it presented. I also LOVED the fact that I won that match 6-4, 6-0, losing just one point in the second set! Overcoming those types of obstacles in such a strong way will even further my love for stress, and THAT is a very important reason for athletes to start this journey of stress-loving soon if they haven't already done so!

My comeback continued into the fall of '23 as a Mansfield tennis friend of mine, Will Calhoun, asked me to compete in some National tournaments with him. I was kind of excited to say yes (knowing that some fears will have to be overcome), and the first tourney was the National Grass Courts in Rhode Island! It was an incredible opportunity as my 20 & 16-year-old boys, Jackson and Mason, live just minutes from the tournament site, and I would get to spend some invaluable time with them (I'm in RI with them about 40 weekends a year, but a week-long stay up there is unique for us!). I also loved that my boys could see their old dad compete on the tennis court a bit, something they really haven't seen much of at all (hard to do if I don't play tennis tournaments, I guess!). Before the tournament began, Mason asked me if I would be nervous. He may have been surprised by my quick yes answer, and he asked me how I would handle that. I explained to him what I do at the beginning of matches. Again, I know myself well so I'm ready for the fearful thoughts that present themselves and at the beginning of a match (or game!) I actually take control of them by actively leading these sorts of thoughts. I actually sort of imagine some of the worst case scenarios and then get myself to realize that even if that all happens, I will still be fine. This helps to calm me down a bit, and then I can move on to battle the task at hand, which in this case was hitting a fuzzy tennis ball off of grass! Btw - Will and I didn't get the result we wanted, but for me, advancing to the quarterfinals of singles and doubles in my first National Tournament in years is something I felt I could be pretty proud of! But more importantly, it reminded me of the benefits of loving the stress, and the value of falling short of hopes - I became super motivated to improve certain aspects of myself so that I could perform even better next time! Apparently sports continue to build character all throughout life!

Life update — *two months later after I had lost 25 pounds, Will and I won a National Title in Philly and ended the year ranked #1 in the country!! Loved the stress!!*

Speaking of character, I wanted to share another story. I played my last soccer game in the ninth grade. Actually, in that last game, I didn't see the field. I had been a back-up goalie for the Junior Varsity team that year, and got to play either goalie or in the field every other game. Now, I'll be the first to admit that I wasn't so good in the field, BUT I was a very good goalie, and I believed I was better than the starter. However, the starter, Larry Delong, was a full-time soccer player and I was a tennis player who played soccer, so even though I had outplayed Larry for years in various soccer leagues, I accepted the back-up role gracefully. Sitting every minute of that last game hit differently though. I would never have quit during any season, but with the season being over, I quickly decided that I was "retiring" from soccer at the age of 14.

My parents accepted this decision but they wanted me to be involved in more sports than just tennis (not surprising from the super-athletic John and Chriss!). So, I chose to run on the cross country team because that was the sport that I believed would most help my tennis. And it did!! During my first season, I made a scheduling mistake and missed a Thursday practice. I called the coach to apologize, and while he accepted, the mistake would come with consequences, and rightfully so! Coach Jay Schmidt reminded me that we had a meet on Saturday and then gave me a choice. He said that because I missed the practice, I would be suspended from that meet. Or, he said, I could make up the practice on Friday (meaning run seven miles before the four-mile practice run Friday) and then become eligible to run in the meet Saturday. Now, I did some quick math. Here was my choice. I could run 11 miles Friday and then another 3.1 on Saturday, or just run the four on Friday and nothing Saturday. What would you do?

I guess I should have mentioned that I HATE running! Why did I choose to run cross country then? Because I'm extremely competitive, that's why! But this was kind of a tough choice. I could run 14.1 miles, or run just four. And as much as I wanted to pick the four, I knew it wasn't the right choice. So, I ran the 11 Friday and then had a painfully slow meet on Saturday. I don't think I was so ready to love the stress at that point, but I did enjoy making the right character choice!

So, why did I make that choice? It may have stemmed from seeing my parents always working hard to be the best at EVERYTHING they were involved in. It also may have stemmed from my dad's attitude about quitting. He simply didn't believe in it! I learned not to either. We will cover that later! But somewhere I learned to love the journey where stress was involved because I knew that stress helped to build character. I knew that stress would help me achieve a higher level of success. Stress is GOOD!! But only if one can learn to love it. I was recently told that the difference between an underachiever and an overachiever is mostly how they respond to a challenge, or respond to stress. Underachievers will try to accomplish a task at hand (aka stressor) two or three times, but if they fail each time, they will give up and walk away. On the other hand, the overachievers may try to overcome that same challenge/task 20 or 30 or even an infinite amount of times before giving up. It's not hard to guess who will be more successful in life.

Are you still not sure that you want to love the stress? Ok, I'll give you two more possible reasons to do so: The first starts with a question. Do you like scary movies? I personally love them! My fiancé, Sharon, hates them! Why does she hate them? I often wonder. I believe it's mostly because of the stress created because of the anticipation of the "jump scares." My favorite movie experience EVER was going with my fiancé, Sharon, and some friends to see Annabelle. What made it so great? Well, it's just a brilliantly made scary movie, but that's not it. What made this movie experience so great was the reaction that Sharon (and then others) had during the scary parts. Everyone in the theater of course jumped when Annabelle (I can only say her name twice because if I say it three times, legend has it that she will appear) popped onto the screen or ran at one of the kids. But Sharon would let out this blood curdling scream that actually would make others around us jump and even scream and gasp themselves! After the super scary moment, we would all giggle and laugh (Sharon too) and Sharon and I would cuddle closer together to get ready for the next one. It was kind of like the thrill of riding a roller coaster. The anticipation and "stress" of climbing up a hill is met with the exhilaration of flying straight down at crazy speeds. To steal a line from the movie "The Girl Next Door," the juice is worth the squeeze. But the juice tastes so much better if you can love the stress.

Ok, last "hard sell" here to get you to love stress: Zack Pasanen was one of the top tennis recruits ever to commit to Brown University to play tennis. One small problem was that he knew it. He came in as a freshman VERY confident and the other guys on the team wanted to "knock him down a peg" at times when this confidence bordered on obnoxiousness. Zack wasn't necessarily irresponsible, but he wasn't as timely as he needed to be. One particular day, he showed up very late to practice, and my assistant, Matt Shaine, and I had exhausted our patience for the tardiness. So, Matt borrowed KG's (Kris Goddard was a junior on the team at the time) bike, and told Zack that he had to run behind him all around the athletic fields and that he must stay within ten yards of the bike at all times. Zack was NOT ready for the toughness this required! Upon return to the courts after Zack failed that task, Matt told Zack that because of the failure and the fact that he essentially quit the challenge, Zack had to do 1000 push-ups. Yes, one thousand! That's not a typo! Do you know how hard it is to do 1000 push-ups? At first Zack thought he was kidding, but the look on Matt's face told him that Matt was dead serious. So, they went out on the field next to the courts and worked on this challenge. Now, I'm sure Zack was very stressed about this. And I know that after completing the 1000 push-ups, he was very sore for a couple of days. But at the end of the day, what is a better story for Zack to tell his grandkids? Would it be better to tell them that his crazy coach asked him to do 1000 push-ups and that he laughed at that and refused to do them? OR, would it be better to tell those grandkids the true story of how he finished those push-ups, that it took him over two hours to do so, that he was sore for days after, and that he was never late to practice again? I'm picking the second one, but I also believe that life is about stories!

CAN TOUGHNESS BE TAUGHT?

Nothing can stop the man with the right mental attitude from achieving his goal; nothing on earth can help the man with the wrong mental attitude.

—*Unknown*

Well, my answer is OF COURSE IT CAN! The challenge of course is: How does a coach do it? Obviously there are a ton of methods aimed at increasing the toughness of a player or a team. Many have seen clips of "toughness gurus" like Bobby Knight (sorry Mike, I know you hate him being an Ohio State fan, but little known fact by some, he DID play for Ohio State! And yes, I know you know that of course!) run his players to the ground while screaming and yelling at them (and yes, maybe sometimes choking them just a little). One coach I learned from at an early age was Bob Huggins (another one of Mike's "favorites!" ha). Huggy Bear was the head basketball coach at the University of Cincinnati when I was playing tennis there and I had the opportunity to actually sit in on some of his practices. Wow, were those intense! I once saw him kick his leading scorer and best player out of practice for turning the ball over ONCE, and that was the day before the team headed to the Final Four! While the screaming techniques were widely publicized (and accepted) in the "olden days" when Mike and I were kids, it is tough to get away with the guerrilla techniques like that today. Part of that reason is that our society has become a lot softer than it was 30 years ago; another reason is likely because coaches are seemingly filmed at all times and their high-paying jobs are on the line every minute, and of course, a bit of it is that many theorists believe that those coaching methods are NOT the best way of producing the healthiest toughness. I as a coach definitely see the benefits of the "tough love" coach. Believe me, I grew up with that and have personally benefited greatly from it! However, I did not necessarily follow that style of coaching as I created my own "bag of tools."

Mike retorts: Point of fact Jay, I think Bob Knight was an amazing coach. I do agree that his style does not transcend time. It should, but it doesn't. Jay got my opinion of Bob Huggins correct though. I see a great difference between being a tough and demanding coach and just being a bully. Demanding a player do things correctly, to be intelligent, to put the team first, and to have the desire to win are great coaching qualities that Coach Knight possessed. Belittling a player to make them obedient is just being a bully. As a coach, Bob Knight was constantly teaching his players the game. He did this aggressively and effectively.

When Coach Knight was at Indiana University he had a number of assistant coaches that would go on to be head coaches. One of these assistants was Dan Dakich. Coach Dakich was at Indiana University for 12 years as an assistant from 1985 to 1997. During a practice Dakich was running a drill. Coach Knight was sitting a few rows up in the bleachers observing the practice. It isn't uncommon for the head coach to turn over running drills to their assistants. Dakich was talking to his groups of players for several minutes and the players weren't understanding how to execute the drill. Coach Knight had enough of this and yelled, "Damn it Dan! If it takes that long to explain, then it's a stupid f'ing drill! Move on!" Coach Knight was demanding of everyone. A bully coach would have just called Coach Dakich some ridiculous insults then yelled at the players for standing around.

Jay adds: Funny story about Dan Dakich – I had the pleasure of working alongside Dan at Bowling Green State University where Dan had his first head coaching position for our basketball program. Dan was an awesome coach in my opinion. He was full of personality and was also extremely smart. Some may see that intelligence in his ESPN commentary during games now. Dan was able to do what very few coaches in any sport could do ... win at Bowling Green. BGSU competed (and still competes) in the Mid-American Conference, and when Dan and I were there, not only was it rated as one of the weakest schools academically in the conference, it easily had the worst overall facilities and paid their coaches the least of all schools in the conference. Those are not necessarily ingredients for winning programs. However, certain coaches at BG were able to overcome these immense obstacles, and Dan was one of them. Oh yeah, back to my "funny story" and the reason I was replying about Dan. Coach Dakich was once telling us a story about playing for Coach Knight at Indiana. He was telling us about a time that they had gotten off the bus after traveling back from an ugly WIN at Iowa. Coach Knight wasn't happy with the play and ordered the entire team back into the gym once they pulled into campus. The team met Coach Knight in the gym and he made them do sprints for an hour straight, up and down the court. Coach Knight then reacted to some mild grumbling from the guys on the team by saying "listen f'ers, you guys are going to keep sprinting until someone has the f'ing guts to push themselves to their limits so hard that they throw up." After running one more sprint, Dan Dakich ran over to the nearest trash can and made himself throw up. The entire team then stared at Coach Knight to see his reaction. Coach looked at Dan, then looked at the team, and then said: "Get the f' out of here." Coach Knight wanted to beat the softness out of his guys, and most times he was successful doing so.

Mike returns: I don't know if Jay's terminology "soft" is the best way to describe society today but there is a great deal of truth to it. For example, a college coach I know was once fired for apparently endangering his players. As a conditioning exercise, he took his team to a public beach with lifeguards, and had his team jog through the water and swim out to a buoy in the public swimming area. A disgruntled player later complained to his wealthy parents, who then complained to the University and the University did what so many do; they protected themselves from a possible negative issue. SOFT. That player probably took their girlfriend to that same beach the next day and I wonder if that Athletic Director took his family there a few times as well to take a little dip in the Atlantic!

Jay volleys back: I once was the youngest Division I head coach in the country of any sport, and as a very young coach, my first real goal was literally "don't mess these guys up too bad!" I knew I had a lot to learn and I knew that I had to sort of "survive" my first couple of years coaching. So, to help me survive, I worked hard to learn from any coach around me and I spent a lot of time at certain coaching conventions listening to many different coaches and taking detailed notes on their topics. One of my favorite coach speeches was given by Coach Chuck Merzbacher, the head women's coach at Ohio State at the time. Chuck was a successful tour player at one point, and in his speech, he was talking about his experiences of how he developed his own high level of toughness. He spoke about how his high-risk game style possibly required a higher level of mental fortitude, and how he worked to develop that. Chuck was a serve and volleyer and he and his coach did a specific drill every Tuesday, and that drill was simply that he had to make 300 volleys in a row into a back box of the tennis court. The box was about 10 x 10 feet, and while that box was definitely big enough for a good volleyer to make pretty consistently, Chuck was definitely a great volleyer. The challenge though wasn't in just hitting it into the box ... it was doing it 300 times without missing! Do you know how long that takes? For Chuck, he would say that he would feel great volleying into those back boxes until he got to about 275, and at that point, his hands definitely started to get a little shaky. At that point in the drill, the fear of course would creep in that if he would miss, he would have to start all the way over again. Chuck said that on some days he could get that done in 30-40 minutes, and other days it took 3-4 hours. Chuck then said that never in his entire pro career did he feel more pressure in a tournament match than he did doing that drill at about 290, and because of the "300s," he was a mental rock in his matches. Hearing that early in my coaching career, I wanted to figure out how to incorporate that into my college team's training.

As I thought about how to do this, I also referenced the experience I had watching my dad coach basketball throughout my childhood. As I have referenced, my dad was definitely a sort of "toughness guru" in that era of coaching, but he didn't just scream and yell. He also mixed in some true mental warfare. He would work to structure his practices to set up tough situations for his team to overcome. For example, I remember a drill he ran often where he had his team set up a particular offensive set. If ANYONE misplayed their position, then the entire team had to run for five minutes. Then they would do it again. To me, it was genius. His team was being forced to learn to deal with some true mental adversity, and they always got stronger because of it.

Thus, I created the "10s." The 10s is a simple tennis drill with many add-ons available. It starts as simply having the player hit 10 balls in a row anywhere into the court while standing around the baseline area. If a player is able to do that with ease, different factors can be added to make the task a bit more challenging. The coach/feeder can add a little pace to the ball coming to the player, can make the ball tougher by mixing the pace more, or hitting more side to side to challenge footwork and even fitness level.

The 10s became a bit of the foundation for an effort of building consistency and toughness for my teams at both Bowling Green and Brown. We would start at least half the practices with the 10s. Sometimes they were cooperative 10s, where each player as they were partnered up almost enabled their partner to get 10 in a row on each side of the court. And we also had competitive 10s, where each player of each pairing was trying to make 10 consecutive balls and get as many 10s as they could get, while making it tough for their partner when it was their turn to try to make them. I also took the 10s with me to New York as I began teaching and coaching at the John McEnroe Tennis Academy.

One of my most interesting examples or memories on court of using the 10s was when I met a 12-year-old boy Daniil. Daniil and his dad came to me for a bit of an introductory trial lesson, for both of us really. They had heard of my coaching background, and also my knowledge of Sport Psychology. Daniil had been struggling emotionally on court mightily, and his dad was looking for someone to help him. So, we went on court for both of us to see what each of us was about. I warmed up with Daniil and then brought out the 10s for our first drill. Daniil's task of course was just to hit 10 balls to one side of the court. Now in the 10s, the coach or player who's counting the player who's trying to get the 10 in a row can sort of make it as easy or tough as they want to. As I was sort of testing Daniil out, I wanted to make it pretty tough for him in the beginning to see how he would respond. Daniil was doing okay but was not able to get the required 10 in a row to accomplish the task. We did this for about five minutes where I made it pretty tough, then I started to soften a little bit at the beginning of the counts. However, once he got to eight or nine, I would hit a ball that would be very difficult for Daniil to return, thus, requiring him to start over.

This was all a bit of a psychological manipulation of course, as I wanted to see how Daniil responded to the frustrations that were of course building. Let's just say he did not respond so well. We stayed on that side for about 20 minutes, and for the last five of those, I was actually trying to make it as easy as possible for him to get to 10 in a row. He finally got the 10, and that meant that all we had to do was just make 10 in a row on the other side of the court. I again raised the difficulty level of the balls I was hitting to him, as I was very interested to see how he would respond to some frustration after he had accomplished half of the task.

Again, his response wasn't so good. He quickly went into a mode where he could probably only see red, and he was rarely getting up to two or three balls in a row into the target area of the court. Then the tea kettle blew over. Daniil missed a ball that would've been the eighth ball in a row as he was trying to get to 10, and his response was to tomahawk his racket into the bench on the side of the court from where he was standing on the baseline. This was about a 40-foot racket toss. The part that I missed here, was that his dad was also sitting on that bench, not only watching this the entire time, but also was forced to dodge the twirling racket as it was barreling towards him. Daniil then went over to the bench, sat down with his dad, and they both simultaneously put their faces into their hands, shaking their heads from side to side.

After a minute to allow the duo to wallow, I gave what I thought was a great speech to try to motivate Daniil to get back on the court, and then asked Daniil: "Would you like to try again?" He replied "No." The 10s showed me very clearly that we had a lot of work to do with Daniil. The ending of the story as we fast forward is an amazing one. Daniil and I spent most of the next three months not practicing on court, but actually doing constructive psychological and emotional control building sessions off court. After a couple months, I allowed us to get on court a little bit and work to add our new set of skills to specific tennis strategy building, working to attach them to his new emotional control skills. Things started looking much better! About a month after our first real tennis lessons on court, Daniil won his first USTA sectional tournament. His dad called me literally in tears thanking me for all the work we had done in the past six months. I should've then called Chuck Merzbacher to thank him for helping me build the 10s. Daniil later went on to win his next two tournaments as well (earning the infamous tournament turkey - I literally delivered a frozen turkey to Daniil at practice after the third title!) and his future continued to impress, winning an NCAA title at Emory University!

The first question of this chapter was: can toughness be taught? I of course believe that process can most definitely be taught, and here is a personal example where my toughness was enhanced with some simple instruction and drilling and maybe a little pain. In the summer of 1990, I just finished my freshman year at Ohio University and tennis-wise, it was not a good year. I had been a very under-control tennis player throughout my junior career, but I went to Ohio University having just had my confidence shaken with a tough loss, the toughest loss of my career, the summer before going to school. My confidence was shaky going into school and it would get exposed in a program that maybe wasn't the best program in the country for me. Our team at Ohio University was very talented, but in the nicest way possible I will say that our coach did little to help our talents shine. He was an old school coach, a coach that would work to break his players down, and then "hope" they would build themselves up.

But his "breaking down methods" were sometimes so ridiculous, that players on the team were seemingly always on the verge of revolt. So, I came back to good ol' Lexington, Ohio that summer, honestly a bit of a mess. Actually, I was a huge mess! It was an important summer tennis-wise for me, because after Ohio University's program was cut that spring, I had chosen to transfer to the University of Cincinnati. Now, what I learned by going to Ohio University was that no matter how good a player may or may not be, that play was going to be evaluated early and possibly harshly by a new coach and by teammates when they arrived on campus. Thus, I needed to have a good summer and prepare for my new school and program. As I returned home, my dad, otherwise known as my coach, told me that he only wanted to see me on court two hours a week. He said that I would be working with him from 6 to 7 PM every Tuesday and Thursday throughout the summer. I said OK! My dad then sort of alluded to what we can call the catch. He said: Jay, for these hours, I only have one rule. That rule is no matter what I ask of you, you have to do it. I didn't really have a choice other than to reply "ok," but I was also desperate to get through my extreme confidence struggles.

The first Tuesday came, and I went to the court at 6 PM. My dad was waiting and he quickly explained the very simple drill that we would be doing. He explained that all we would be doing was hitting up in the middle of the court for an hour straight. He said we would hit down the middle for this hour, and every time I miss, I would just have to do five push-ups. A couple of thoughts ran into my head quickly. Number one, as much as I love my dad and believe he's an amazing coach, his tennis skills are only "pretty good," meaning he wasn't the most consistent hitter, so hitting up the middle wasn't really something that I would ever expect. I knew that he would be hitting balls all over the court, and probably outside the court. The second thought was that I wasn't so sure I could make three or four balls in a row without missing myself even if the ball was hit to me in the middle of the court. That's really how bad of a mess I was! So I started to calculate in my head in the span of an hour, how many push-ups would I actually be doing. I honestly wasn't sure, but I anticipated it would be a lot!

The first hour was tough, as I estimated that I did about 600 push-ups after missing a lot of balls. But that wasn't the toughest of the hours. After that first session, I woke up the next day and couldn't straighten my arms. My chest was in so much pain that if the wind blew it would almost make me go down to a knee. On the second day after this initial session I woke up hoping it might be a little better; it was actually worse. Then I remembered it was Thursday, our second session day. So, I went to the court that day to meet my dad and he again reiterated the simple drill that we were going to do. Five push-ups for every miss. I don't remember a lot of that other than being in a lot of pain for about 52 of the 60 minutes. I could barely feel my arms after about the first 25 push-ups, and probably ended up doing another 500 that hour. Now I won't lie, I doubt very many of those push-ups were quality push-ups, but I still did them. The next week was a little better although still very painful, and then in about week four, I hit a turning point. I stopped worrying about missing and started to think of things to put into my mind that allowed me to simply make more balls. I started thinking about my feet and the energy I was putting into each movement and then I started feeling more and more comfortable with my stroke mechanics to the point where instead of trying to figure out how I was swinging, I just started thinking of where I wanted to hit the ball - like exactly the spot on the court. In week six and seven I started to feel great. My confidence had returned. I felt like I could make almost every ball and during week eight I played a tournament where I dominated, barely missing the entire weekend. That continued into week 10 and in our first lesson of that week, my goal was literally not to miss the ball for an entire hour. I went 52 minutes and I can remember this like it was yesterday. I got a little bit of a bad bounce on a ball and my feet got a touch lazy. I hit a forehand and I missed it right on top of net tape. If I hit up on that ball just a fraction more, then it goes in; however, tennis is a game of inches. I missed that ball, went down and did my five push-ups, and then got ready for the next ball, well sorta. My dad fed the next one, and I missed another forehand! I immediately said something to myself that wasn't so nice, did my five push-ups, and then got a lot more focused for the last seven or so minutes. Those two were the only two balls I missed in that hour. I went to school a week later prepared to play on my new team and because of that simple drill, because of the toughness development that drill caused, my tennis career literally turned around. I spent three years playing at the University of Cincinnati and my senior year I was a First Team All-Conference performer after winning over 100 matches in my college career. I was proud of my college career, proud of my dad as a coach, and forever my mind-set was changed because of that simple drill.

CAN TOUGHNESS BE TAUGHT?

Recently, as a tennis coach for a lot of great junior players, I thought of bringing back a certain set of drills that could mesh the spirit of the 10s with my dad's incredible summer hour-long drills, in an effort to help TEACH TOUGHNESS to my players.

So, without further ado, HERE is :

JAY'S 101 LEVELS OF TOUGHNESS

Level 1: 10s full court, coach pushes
Level 2: 10s full court, coach rips
Level 3: 10s into 1 side - coach pushes
Level 4: 10s into 1 side - coach rips
Level 5: 10s over service line, full court, coach pushes
Level 6: 10s over service line, full court, coach rips
Level 7: 10s over service line and rope, full court, coach pushes
Level 8: 10s over service line and rope, full court, coach rips
Level 9: 10s over the service line, 1 side, coach pushes
Level 10: 10s over service line, 1 side, coach rips
Level 11: 10s over service line and rope, 1 side, coach pushes
Level 12: 10s over service line and rope, 1 side, coach rips
Level 13: 5-10s over 60-foot line, full court, coach pushes
Level 14: 5-10s over 60-foot line, full court, coach rips
Level 15: 5-10s over 60-foot line, 1 side, coach pushes
Level 16: 5-10s over 60-foot line, 1 side, coach rips
Level 17: 10s over service line and under & over the rope, full court, coach pushes
Level 18: 10s over service line and under rope, full court, coach pushes
Level 19: 10s over service line and under & over rope, full court, coach rips
Level 20: 10s over service line and under rope, full court, coach rips
Level 21: 10s full court, coach pushes, punish every miss
Level 22: 10s full court, coach rips, punish every miss
Level 23: 10s into 1 side, coach pushes, punish every miss (i.e. sprint/pushups)
Level 24: 10s into 1 side, coach rips, punish every miss

Level 25: 10s over service line, full court, coach pushes, punish every miss

Level 26: 10s over service line, full court, coach rips, punish every miss

Level 27: 10s over service line and rope, full court, coach pushes, punish every miss

Level 28: 10s over service line and rope, full court, coach rips, punish every miss

Level 29: 10s over service line and under & over the rope, full court, coach rips, punish every miss

Level 30: 10s over service line and under rope, full court, coach rips, punish every miss

Level 31: 10s over service line, 1 side coach pushes, punish every miss

Level 32: 10s over service line, 1 side, coach rips, punish every miss

Level 33: 10s over service line and rope, 1 side, coach pushes, punish every miss

Level 34: 10s over service line and rope, 1 side, coach rips, punish every miss

Level 35: 10s over service line and under & over the rope, 1 side, coach rips, punish every miss

Level 36: 10s over service line and under the rope, 1 side, coach rips, punish every miss

Level 37: 5-10s over 60-foot line, full court, coach pushes, punish every miss

Level 38: 5-10s over 60-foot line, full court, coach rips, punish every miss

Level 39: 5-10s over 60-foot line, 1 side, coach pushes, punish every miss

Level 40: 5-10s over 60-foot line, 1 side, coach rips, punish every miss

Level 41: 5-10s over 60-foot line and rope, 1 side, coach rips, punish every miss

Level 42: 5-10s over 60-foot line and under & over the rope, 1 side, coach rips, punish every miss

Level 43: 5-10s over 60-foot line and under the rope, 1 side, coach rips, punish every miss

Level 44 plus: Make all above 5-10s "competitive" (players battle for the most 10s)

Level 45: Groundstroke game to 11, punish every miss

Level 46: Groundstroke game to 11, student hits every ball cross, punish every miss

Level 47: Super tiebreaker, punish every miss

Level 48: Super tiebreaker, one serve only, punish every miss

Level 49: Super tiebreaker, student hits every ball cross, punish every miss

Level 50: Super tiebreaker, one serve only, student hits every ball cross, punish every miss

Level 51: 1 set, punish every miss

Level 52: 1 set, every game starts at 30-all, punish every miss

Level 53: 1 set, every game starts at 30-all, one serve only, punish every miss

Level 54: 1 set, every game starts at 30-all, student hits every ball cross, punish every miss

Level 55: 1 set, every game starts at 30-all, one serve only, student hits every ball cross, punish every miss

Level 56: 2 out of 3 sets, punish every miss

Level 57: 2 out of 3 sets, every game starts at 30-all, punish every miss

Level 58: 2 out of 3 sets, one serve only, every game starts at 30-all, punish every miss

Level 59: 2 out of 3 sets, every game starts at 30-all, student hits every ball cross, punish every miss

Level 60: 2 out of 3 sets, every game starts at 30-all, one serve only, student hits every ball cross, punish every miss

Level 61: 5-25 min, full court, coach pushes, punish every miss

Level 62: 30min-1 hour, full court, coach pushes, punish every miss (DAD DRILL)

Level 63: 5-25 min, full court, coach rips, punish every miss

Level 64: 30min-1 hour, full court, coach rips, punish every miss

Level 65: 5-25 min, 1 side, coach pushes, punish every miss

Level 66: 30min-1 hour, 1 side, coach pushes, punish every miss

Level 67: 5-25 min, 1 side, coach rips, punish every miss

Level 68: 30min-1 hour, 1 side, coach rips, punish every miss

Level 69: 5-25 min, over service line, full court, coach pushes, punish every miss

Level 70: 30min-1 hour, over service line, full court, coach pushes, punish every miss

Level 71: 5-25 min, over service line, full court, coach rips, punish every miss

Level 72: 30min-1 hour, over service line, full court, coach rips, punish every miss

Level 73: 5-25 min, 1 side over service line, coach pushes, punish every miss

Level 74: 30min-1 hour, 1 side over service line, coach pushes, punish every miss

Level 75: 5-25 min, 1 side over service line, coach rips, punish every miss

Level 76: 30min-1 hour, 1 side over service line, coach rips, punish every miss

Level 77: 5-25 min, 1 side, over rope, coach pushes, punish every miss

Level 78: 30min-1 hour, 1 side, over rope, coach pushes, punish every miss

Level 79: 5-25 min, 1 side, over rope, coach rips, punish every miss

Level 80: 30min-1 hour, 1 side, over rope, coach rips, punish every miss

Level 81: 5-25 min, 1 side, over rope, over service line, coach pushes, punish every miss

Level 82: 30min-1 hour, 1 side, over rope, over service line, coach pushes, punish every miss

Level 83: 5-25 min, 1 side over service line, over rope, coach rips, punish every miss

Level 84: 30min-1 hour, 1 side over service line, over rope, coach rips, punish every miss

Level 85: 5-25 min, 1 side, under & over rope, coach pushes, punish every miss

Level 86: 30min-1 hour, 1 side, under & over rope, coach pushes, punish every miss

Level 87: 5-25 min, 1 side, under & over the rope, coach rips, punish every miss

Level 88: 30min-1 hour, 1 side, under & over the rope, coach rips, punish every miss

Level 89: 5-25 min, 1 side, under rope coach pushes, punish every miss

CAN TOUGHNESS BE TAUGHT?

Level 90: 30min-1 hour, 1 side, under rope, coach pushes, punish every miss

Level 91: 5-25 min, 1 side, under rope coach rips, punish every miss

Level 92: 30min-1 hour, 1 side, under rope, coach rips, punish every miss

Level 93: 5-25 min, 1 side over 60-foot line, coach pushes, punish every miss

Level 94: 5-25 min, 1 side over 60-foot line, coach rips, punish every miss

Level 95: 5-25 min, 1 side over 60-foot line, over the rope, coach rips, punish every miss

Level 96: 30min-1 hour, 1 side, over 60-foot line, coach rips, punish every miss

Level 97: 5-25 min, 1 side, over 60-foot line, under rope, coach rips, punish every miss

Level 98: 30min-1 hour, 1 side, over service line, under rope, coach rips, punish every miss

Level 99: 30min-1 hour, 1 side, over 60-foot line, over the rope, coach rips, punish every miss

Level 100: 30min-1 hour, 1 side, over 60-foot line, under & over rope, coach rips, punish every miss

Level 101: 30min-1 hour, 1 side, over 60-foot line, under rope, coach rips, punish every miss

Mike chimes in: I am not sure if Jay's practice regimen is an example of toughness. It is definitely a method to increase skill, endurance, and determination. All coaches should develop the 10s to fit their sport. It isn't a useful tool; it is a vital tool. The coach also needs to have the determination to see it through. When the player starts the inevitable meltdown when the drill becomes difficult, the coach cannot let the player off. If the coach relents then the whole drill was a waste.

I view toughness with a different lens. The athlete that gets to level 101 will certainly win more matches than they lose, but what happens when they step on a tennis ball and twist their ankle? Do they give up and forfeit the match or do they fight through pain and continue to play? I subscribe to the John Wayne motto of "being scared to death but saddling up anyway." Pain is nothing more than an obstacle to overcome. Too many athletes choose not to overcome obstacles. They see an obstacle as a barrier.

I was watching the World Series about 30 years ago. I was excited because my roommate was a big fan of one of the teams playing in it and it was an Ohio team. Unfortunately, professional Ohio teams haven't played for many championships in my lifetime. During the pregame hoopla they announced that one of the star players wouldn't be playing that day. Then they announced what exactly his injury was and I was beyond disappointed. I didn't even watch the game. The team's star player was sitting out the game because he had a hangnail, a gosh darn hangnail! I don't know for sure how hard that particular player practiced his entire life, but I have to believe he worked hard. To get to that level, the player had to put the time and effort into it, but the guy threw it all away on a hangnail. It may have been the most painful hangnail of all time, but players play.

I don't know if that World Series game was the very beginning of teaching softness, but at the very least it was in its infancy. I remember listening to an interview with Charles Barkley (one of my favorite athletes of all time). During the interview Barkley said "he wasn't a role model." I am sorry Chuck - you don't get to decide that. Everybody has the potential to be a role model. Top athletes or the next door neighbor can be a role model at any given time. A person can't control who is watching them or who wants to be like them. It just happens. Young athletes watch, they observe, and then they emulate the behaviors of their sport's heroes. So, when a young athlete sees a Major League baseball player remove himself from the lineup for a hangnail, that athlete may emulate that. Steph Curry is constantly chomping on his mouthpiece. If you go to any high school basketball game today, you will see several players chomping on their mouthpieces.

In the NFL, more and more players are sitting out games for injuries that 20 years ago wouldn't have been noted in injury reports. Players don't want to play a game if they aren't 100 percent. A bad game can lower stats and potentially hurt contract negotiations. In the NBA, LeBron James has made load management a topic. Players are sitting out games during the regular season to save themselves for postseason play. This may be a smart move but it doesn't demonstrate toughness.

The player who goes through Jay's 101 levels and then plays a match through injuries and all obstacles is a tough player. I have been a lifelong Cleveland Browns fan. I started watching football when the Kardiac Kids were so exciting to watch; however, the painful fumble, the agonizing drive, and all the mediocrity of the last two decades scarred many of us. The Browns finally seem now to be on the right track. They made the playoffs during the 2020-2021 season. The 2022 season started with high expectations. Then life happened. Injuries to players on both sides of the ball, Covid protocols, terrible officiating, poor play execution, poor play calling, and mistake after mistake riddled the franchise. There are a couple players that kept me watching though. I love the way Nick Chubb plays but more so, I like the way he conducts himself with class. Then there is Baker Mayfield. In 2020-2021 he was everyone's favorite player and then, in 2021-2022 he was getting booed. Mayfield suffered a shoulder injury that required surgery; then he had a foot injury, and the Browns essentially sent out a different offensive line every week all while the receiving corps went through injury after injury as well. Yet Mayfield suited up every week and played harder and harder each game. Baker Mayfield is a tough player.

This paragraph is not trying to decide who is better, Michael Jordan or LeBron James, but I have to say that I believe the notion of load management is the opposite of toughness. I can provide numerous examples of how tough Michael Jordan is, but I am going with the best. During the 1997 NBA Finals Jordan either had the flu or food poisoning (watch The Last Dance, ESPN). Everyone advised him to sit out of the game that evening, but Jordan played. Even if he didn't play well in the game, he still played. His stat line was 38 points, 7 rebounds, 5 assists, and 3 steals. That is pretty darn good.

Jordan played in the game not because it was the NBA Finals; he played because he is a phenomenal competitor. LeBron James didn't coin the phrase load management but he made it cool (not really). LeBron has had his share of toughness showings. In the 2015 NBA Finals, LeBron put on a clinic of toughness. There were many story lines throughout the series. The Cavs had many injuries and few All-Stars, compared to the star studded Warrior lineup. LeBron had the series of his career. He was determined and tough. It was one of the most impressive performances ever. I was truly inspired by his effort. The Cavs came up a little short in this series. However, they came back and won a championship the following season. I remember LeBron's performance in the losing series of 2015. I cannot recall one of his plays in the 2016 winning series. I love toughness. It inspires, it wins, it transcends time. When a player voluntarily takes themselves out of the lineup they are rejecting toughness. Players play.

> **Jay agrees here:** I DO! 100% spot on! Players freaking play!! But Mike, you don't remember "the block" by LeBron in game seven of the 2016 finals? Come on bra!!

Mike is back: Okay Jay, maybe I remember THAT play! LeBron James uses all of modern science to get himself conditioned to play. He drinks all of the healthy juices and sports drinks. He has a nutritionist control his diet and workouts. After games he uses full-body cryotherapy. Apparently, LeBron James spends $1.5 million dollars on his body each year. Michael Jordan smoked cigars pregame and recovered from the game with some bourbon. Why was Jordan able to play a full load of games and LeBron not? LeBron James is physically strong, yet he believes in load management. Maybe the better way to research the difference between Michael Jordan and LeBron James is to look at Jordan's college experience. Or, we can study their high school experiences as they were very different. Somewhere Jordan was taught toughness. In many ways LeBron James is a great role model, but he is teaching softness. Just as toughness can be taught, so can softness.

As a basketball coach I was constantly amazed by injuries my players would incur. I had this one player, Craig, who constantly battled an ankle injury. That type of injury is very common in basketball. What was amazing is that this particular player had an injured ankle when he was on defense but not on offense. On offense, Craig never seemed to limp around the court but he certainly limped all the way down the court getting back on defense. When he made a basket the limp was even more dramatic. I didn't view Craig as tough.

> **Jay concludes:** I think we've all played with a Craig!! And I'm not talking about you here Craig Nisgor, so don't worry!! That actually reminds me of a quick story! When I was coaching at Brown, I would play noon hoops with a bunch of other Brown coaches and some alumni every Tuesday and Thursday at a "certain time." That was before some complete idiot Brown U administrator decided that he didn't want the University to be liable for any injuries that might occur and he shut it down. How soft!! Omg. Okay, back to my story. A friend of mine and our assistant swim coach, Craig Nisgor, started to come and play in these games, but he was bad. He was an essential basketball beginner and he moved like a swimmer. Ok, maybe some swimmers can run fast, but I'm sure the point is received here! Craig played in the game and he loved it. But he was bad. So, what did he do? He asked me if we could grab two other coaches and play two on two on Wednesdays! And that's what we did every week for a year, often with my good friend and incredible wrestling coach, John Clark! Instead of quitting or being soft and sort of being content just sucking on Tuesdays and Thursdays, Craig went to work, and he got better! Craig got SO much better that a year later he was starting on our intramural team, the Rousters, and if I'm not mistaken, we were the champions! But of course, life is all about stories. Thanks Mike for the Craig reference!

Mike responds: You're welcome Jay.

CONFIDENCE IS THE KEY

Confidence doesn't come out of nowhere. It's a result of something... hours and days and weeks and years of constant work and dedication.

—Roger Staubach

I nervously walked into my interview at Bowling Green State University when I realized something. If the BG Directors were considering me at the age of 24 on par so to speak with the other more experienced coaches set to interview with them, then I wondered if they thought of not just how good I was at that moment, but how good I would be in five years. My thought was that if it was safe to assume that my speed of coaching skill growth would be much more rapid than those coaches (partially because I knew so little!), then if we were similar now, that meant that I would be a much better coach than the other candidates five years down the road! Now, I just had to sell that to the hiring committee!

So, I sat down and they asked me to start and after I introduced myself and thanked them for having me I said this: "I want to let everyone know that I AM 24 years old and there are two things I want to assure you in regards to that. First, I WILL get older!" They all chuckled. Thank goodness they accepted my humor! "And second," I said, "I am certain that you have two other great coaching candidates and I know that they must be very solid coaches. However, I want you to think of this. IF you classify me as a coach who currently is at or very close to the level of those more experienced and older coaches, I would ask you who you might guess will be the better coach in five years? Will it be the coach who has had a lot of years under his belt and who has already learned a majority of the information he will gather in his career, OR would it be the young coach who will learn a TON in just the next couple of years and with that rapid learning curve will become a FAR better coach than he is today. Which coach will be better?"

Mike jumps in: Jay shared a great example of self-confidence. Sometimes we confuse self-confidence with arrogance; they are very different concepts. I have tried for many years to teach my players the difference between being confident and being cocky. When a player walks onto the field, court, or course, coaches want players to be confident. The big question is how do you teach confidence? In golf, I had a transition season. The previous season my team had qualified for the State Tournament and we set many school records. That particular team was loaded with seniors. So, I knew the upcoming season my team was going to lack experience and self-confidence. I spent the summer before the season reading books on sports psychology and playing with confidence. I really enjoyed Bob Rotella's book *Golf is a Game of Confidence*. I highly recommend it to all players and coaches (after you finish this book!).

What I learned is that a player can't simply tell themselves that they are good, and confidence happens. Self-confidence is achieved through a series of positive events. I watch a lot of different sports on television and I constantly hear broadcasters talk about a player's state of mind. In football, coaches often try to call the simplest pass plays at the beginning of a game to give the quarterback easy throws to make. This should allow a quarterback to build self-confidence and therefore have a great game. But, what happens if those easy throws get intercepted by the defense because everyone on the planet knows the quarterback isn't going deep on the first throw of the game. The quarterback needs to build self-confidence in practice. Hoping a quarterback can grow confidence after a couple screen-plays or quick slants is a disaster waiting to happen.

When I watch basketball and a player is struggling shooting from the perimeter inevitably the analyst will suggest taking the ball to the rack. This action can have four possible outcomes. The player could get all the way to the basket and make the layup, or the player could get fouled and earn a trip to the foul line. The analyst is predicting that if the player sees the ball go through the hoop, then they will gain self-confidence. A third outcome could be that they get all the way to the basket and miss the layup, and the fourth is that the player could be fouled but then miss the free throw attempts. Again, self-confidence is acquired in practice. Now can one made free throw trigger self-confidence? The answer is a conditional YES.

The title of Rotella's book is fantastic. I don't know if truer words have ever been written. Golf is definitely a game of confidence. In golf there are so many things to challenge a player's confidence. A player can hit a great shot but that shot ends up in a divot, or takes a bad bounce and finds a penalty area. A player can hit a putt on the perfect line but it hits a poorly repaired mark and falls off line. One of the worst blows to a golfer's confidence is the dreaded lip out. The lip out is dreaded because a player can't get any closer to making the shot only to have to hit another putt. A couple lip outs in a round can really derail a player's confidence. The shame of these scenarios is the player's state of mind. Instead of focusing on how well the player hit the putt they only see the result of a missed putt. I have heard countless television analysts describe a struggling golfer's confidence. After one or two lip outs the analyst will say, "they just need to see one go in and everything will be ok." I am not sure this is accurate. Making a putt does not grow self-confidence.

In golf, I have watched many players struggle on the greens during a tournament. I approach the struggling player and ask them how they are doing, and I almost always get the same response. "I am hitting the ball great but I just can't score." I ask a simple follow-up question, "why can't you score?" The player answers, "I just can't get anything to go in." The reason they can't get anything to go in is usually a lack of confidence. During a tournament it is really hard to build confidence in a player's mind. So, I try to use little tricks to get them to not think about all of the missed putts. I may suggest moving the ball forward in their stance, or moving it back in their stance. I may suggest trying to relax their hands after they grip the putter, or I may suggest a small change in their routine. I don't make these suggestions because they absolutely need to do them because they have a flaw. I do it to change their focus. My main goal at this point is to get them through the round without further diminishing their confidence. The real confidence building takes place after the round.

A coach should include confidence building into every practice. Jay's 10s drill is a great way to do this. Of course a coach will use the concept and adapt the drill to their sport and level of player. In 2022, I had a pretty good golf team with some skilled players. In the offseason I had individual lessons with each player where we focused mostly on the full swing. Once the season started and we met as a team, we never worked on the full swing. I told the team if they wanted to bash golf balls to get to the range before or after practice. The scheduled practice time was for short game work and confidence. We have 90-minute practices, which are dedicated to improving a player's short game and confidence. In golf the short game includes putting, chip shots and pitch shots. Every drill we do is a competitive drill. Every drill has winners and losers. I will set up a putting drill that has a points system. For example, a player will putt a ball from 25 feet. Any ball that is short of the hole is a minus three; a made putt is worth five points. A putt that stops one foot beyond the hole is a plus three; a ball that stops within two feet behind the hole is a plus two; and a ball that stops within three feet is a plus one. Then I will place two tees in the green about two inches apart. The player has to hit a putt from six feet between the tees to earn another three points. Finally, the player has to make a three foot uphill and straight putt to keep any of the points they earned. Players will make five circuits of the three shots accumulating the points each round. Whomever has the most points is the winner. The rest of the team has to do some form of physical exercise for not winning. I tell my players this drill is to teach them distance control, which it does. However, it is really a confidence drill. The final three-foot putt is the confidence builder. If you recall the second putt is a putt between two tees two inches apart. The diameter of a golf hole is 4 ¼ inches. I shrink the target by half and this gets them focusing on a very small target. So when the player moves onto the next putt, the hole seems larger than it is. Making the final putt is the confidence builder.

> **Jay adds:** I love the mix of games and goals used in this putting game and I also love the production of pressure, especially because the presence of pressure in this game is aimed to build confidence. Watching my dad coach basketball at a young age gave me all sorts of free coaching lessons really, and one of those was the way he operated the end of just about every practice. He wanted the players to walk back into the locker room feeling a bit beat up for sure, but also it was obvious that he wanted them feeling stronger, and thus more confident in their abilities to perform well and overcome obstacles. One example of this was his simple "free-throw drill." For the last section of at least one practice per week, Coach Harris would have his squad line up around the key, and one by one, they would go up to the line with the simple task of making one free throw. The goal was for the team, one player at a time, to make ten straight shots, but every miss would result in a team sprint. The sprint was the "produced pressure," and the goal of enhanced confidence was felt every time that last player hit the 10th shot. Now, there were times that this exercise would go on longer than any of the players hoped, and those sessions actually produced the most stress, and thus, the largest enhancement of confidence. As I have said, stress is a great tool, and in the most stressful of free throw sessions where the team had to run and run and run as the missed free throws added up, the feeling felt when that 10th free throw hit the bottom of the net was borderline euphoric, and not only did that clutch player attain a greater level

of confidence in himself, but the entire team also became more confident in him, and about themselves as well.

I learned the importance of confidence at a very young age, and as I aged, I needed all of it to compete in the sport I loved, tennis. Mike, close your eyes and ears here for a second. Ha! Tennis is an amazing sport because it REQUIRES confidence! Singles players are out there all by themselves, and they are constantly asking the question, "can I win?" If they can get to the point where they truly believe they can, then most likely, they will. I was a tiny tennis player in high school. At the end of my junior year, I was still only 5'6" and about 120 pounds (I'm 6'4" 220 now! And yes Mike, I know I need to lose 20 more!!). As a munchkin tennis player, everyone I played was bigger, and there were times that I questioned how I could beat these bigger dudes. But then one day, I was competing with a kid almost a foot taller than me and the football team walked by the courts and saw the ridiculous size difference. They stayed to watch for a while and started cheering me on (and maybe threatening my opponent a little). This support literally made me feel taller than my opponent and I ended up crushing the kid! That night, I wrote on a small piece of paper, "confidence is the key," and I tacked it on my bulletin board. It's still on that same bulletin board today!

As I learned how to control my own confidence, I became much more powerful on the court. I really became my own coach. When thoughts would pop into my head, I would work to only let the ones that would add to my confidence slip past my brain's filter. The bad ones would mostly get discarded like trash. I learned that confidence is ultimately only controlled by one thing, and that is the person choosing to be or not to be confident.

One of my favorite players ever, Kris Goddard (first team All-Ivy) once walked up to me during a Brown University tennis practice and said: "Coach, I don't feel confident." I quickly responded: "Kris, I want to punch you in the face." Kris's expression was like: WTF! I then explained: "Kris, when you admit that you are not confident, then in my mind, you have essentially quit! You have decided to stop trying to control your confidence and I guess just let fate take over?" I added: "Confidence is the one thing you have 100% control over. YOU, as an athlete, get to choose how to feel. You get to work hard to build physical, mental and emotional skills to prepare you to be a great competitor, and then when in the moments inside the arena, you get to choose what thoughts will slip into the area of your brain that controls the expectations of what is going to happen, or in another word, confidence."

I had an amazing set of twins essentially fall into my lap at Bowling Green. Nicolas and Micael Lopez-Acevedo came to BG on an academic and cultural scholarship. They were from Puerto Rico and they were darn good tennis players. This was the first set of twins I had ever coached (I've coached a few others since!) and it was super interesting. They would finish each other's sentences and pick up for each other. For example, Nico lost his wallet at least once a week but Micael always found it. And Micael would lose focus in class and forget to take notes, but Nico would have it all written. It was almost like they had one complete personality in two bodies! On the tennis court it was similar. Nico was super solid and cautious with no real ability to take risks, whereas Micael had all kinds of power and wasn't afraid to be a risk-taker, but he had no control of his emotions. In an off-court session with Micael, I once asked him: "what is the percentage of thoughts that soak into your focus during a match that helps you, and what percentage hurts you?" He was super honest and estimated that 10% helped him and 90% hurt him. I then asked him if he thought it would be good if he could get to 50/50. He just smiled, I think hoping I had a magic pill to give him. While there wasn't a "magic pill," we got to work. I got Micael to first realize that HE did have control over the thoughts by understanding that his brain was a literal filter that could be trained to allow helpful thoughts to sink in while pushing bad thoughts away. I showed him how well he could play when allowing the helpful thoughts to occupy his focus, and I got him to learn to replace the damaging thoughts with either positive or constructive thoughts. After a month of constant mental work, Micael got to 50/50, and by no coincidence, went from our #8 guy to our #5 guy, and helped us have a great season!

Notice that Micael didn't get to 100% helpful thoughts! I actually don't think that is possible, and I also believe that it's damaging to strive for that. What is important is for an athlete to be honest with themselves in regards to where their own percentages are at, and then work to develop the skills to improve those percentages. I think the best competitors can control it so well that they are likely close to 90 to 10, but even the best can't prevent doubts from creeping in.

Mike adds: Hopefully, everyone catches that sentence of "after a month of constant mental work." Confidence is not achieved by a single coaching trick. It is achieved by solid coaching and practice over a period of time. What makes everything go a little easier is when the player recognizes their own negative self-talk, and wants to reduce it.

I want to share an example of how a coach can very easily hurt a player's confidence. I had a former player, Alaina, go on to play at Ashland University. AU is a Division II university in north central Ohio. The coach at AU stayed in constant contact with her during the summer before her freshman season. Alaina did everything that the coach asked her to do. She was very excited for the start of the season. The coach had a policy that every player had to qualify for every tournament, which is an awesome policy. Alaina was ready for the challenge. She qualified in fourth position for the first tournament. This was a real confidence builder for her. The confidence carried over to day one of the tournament. She was third on her team, and the team was in the top five. If every player on the team just shaved a stroke or two off their score for the final round, AU would win the tournament.

I made the trip to Youngstown for the final round. Alaina was bubbling with excitement. It had been a while since I saw her that excited to play a round of golf. Unfortunately, round two did not get off to a great start. She made a bogey on the first hole and then a double bogey, and she was starting to run a little red. She made a par on the third hole and I thought that might calm her down. The coach showed up at this point and had a quick chat with Alaina. He told her that she needed to make pars. This was the first mistake. A college player knows what score they need to shoot. This little comment by the coach essentially tempted an onset of negative self-talk. Questions flooded into Alaina's mind like: "what did he mean by that? Does he think I am doing bad? Am I letting the team down? Is he mad at me?"

Alaina then made more bogies and double-bogies, and the round unraveled. Mistake number two was that the coach didn't return to Alaina for over two hours. When he did return he just brought her a box lunch. College tournaments have live scoring, so the coach knew she was doing poorly but decided to spend time watching his number one player. Alaina finished in fifth place on her team and the team dropped in the standings.

Mistake number three was that the coach didn't have qualifying for the next tournament and chose not to take Alaina. Instead, he sent her with the B team. Not surprisingly, she didn't do well. The fall season did not meet Alaina's expectations. The coach said to her multiple times that "he hadn't given up on her." I disagree with the coach and so did Alaina. Mistake number four was that the coach had determined who would travel to the first three tournaments of the spring season, and Alaina was not included in the tournaments. The coach had abandoned his policy of qualifying for tournaments and went to coach's pick. Many sports are very subjective, but golf and tennis are not among them. A basketball coach has to assess a player's practice performance and game performance to determine who plays and who sits. Golf is about the numbers. I commended the AU coach for using qualifying rounds to determine his lineup, but he abandoned it after one tournament.

I like Alaina's grit. The first tournament that she would be able to play in was at the University of Kentucky's golf course in late March. She spent all winter working on her game. She was using JR Ables as her swing coach. He worked in Columbus, Ohio, and was the former OSU Women's coach. He is a great swing coach and he unknowingly was building Alaina's confidence. Alaina drove an hour through a snowstorm to make it to a lesson. The lesson was the best thing to happen to Alaina's confidence. After a few swings, JR said to her that everything looked perfect. He just sat back and watched her hit ball after ball. Alaina was filled with confidence. That lesson was on a Saturday afternoon. The following Monday she had practice with her team. Before practice began she chatted with the AU coaching staff about her previous lesson. As the team practice began Alaina was hitting some really good shots. The assistant coach was there and watching her and approached her and said, "we still need to change your grip. You are not doing what I want with your hands." Mistake five!

I want to avoid the conversation about the qualifications of JR over the assistant coach, who is all about technology teaching the golf swing. Why in the world would any coach question a player who is beaming with confidence and playing well? All the hard work that Alaina put in, and all of the hard work of JR was now in jeopardy. Alaina called me when the practice was over and described the situation to me. I knew very well what was at stake. So, I had to dig deep into my sport psychology book to find the perfect thing to restore her confidence quickly. I said to Alaina, "that coach is a freaking moron."

Jay chuckles: Out loud actually as I read that! Ha

Mike continues: I don't really think the assistant coach is a moron. However, in one little sentence, that coach could have undone all the great work Alaina and JR had done. My "moron" comment was searching for a laugh and to get her to not put too much stock into

CONFIDENCE IS THE KEY

his comment about her grip. The assistant coach had an opportunity to make Alaina into a confidence monster, but he took a different approach. If the assistant coach would have just watched Alaina hit and applauded her work, then he could have elevated her confidence.

After a few moments of laughter with Alaina I then explained why the assistant coach might have made that dreadful comment. Coaches want to help players. He had an idea of what he wanted Alaina's swing to look like and apparently her hands weren't matching that idea. So, he wanted to do something he felt would help her. Another possibility was that the assistant coach wanted to be "The Man." Coaches have egos too and they can be very fragile. There is a chance that the assistant coach was threatened by JR. By commenting on Alaina's grip he may have tried to undermine JR's work in an effort to make himself look better. When I am working with a player I constantly preach about the needs of the team, which hopefully the reader understands by now. My duty is to the player and if a coach is doing something to hinder the player's performance I always side with the player. I do this because a young player's confidence level is more fragile and detrimental to performance than the coach's ego.

Coaches need to be very careful when to be a skills coach and when to be a mental coach. Never let ego enter into coaching. A good coach should surround themselves with as many great coaches as possible. If a player is struggling with a skill and is underperforming, then a coach should step in and offer swing advice. If the player feels good about their swing, a good coach should get the heck out of the way.

> **Jay quickly concludes:** "Confidence is the key" - that is what I wrote on a piece of paper and tacked to my bulletin board that was hung in every college dorm room of mine. I read that note hundreds of times, and I believe strongly in it to this day. What Mike mentioned at the end of his diatribe here is so important. Coaches need to know when to work on physical skills and when to work on the mental and emotional side. It is one of the toughest balances to achieve, but is likely the most important coaching skill

the great ones possess. I recently received this compliment from the parent of one of my most promising players, *"Thanks Jay. She always walks off the court with more confidence after she spends time with you. That may be your best gift."* Balance achieved!

BOOM MENTALITY

You can't half-ass your way through life and ever expect to get anywhere.

—Donna Rimmer

Jay starts: Mike and I both grew up eating and breathing tons and tons of sports. We both became huge sports fans of certain teams, and while we both, as northern Ohio kids, grew up being inflicted with the pain caused from being a Cleveland Browns, Cavs and Indians fan, we both did have some highlights with our teams here and there. I was also a Reds fan as a kid, so I got to experience two championships with the Big Red Machine in the mid-70s, although I was really young. Then, while living in Cincinnati, I was lucky enough to experience the 1990 World Series Champion Reds with Eric Davis, Paul O'Neal, Chris Sabo, José Rio and the "Nasty Boys." I was a sophomore at the University of Cincinnati at the time, and that was just an awesome experience to be in the city while the team became the world champions. But for both Mike and I, I'm not sure if we'd ever experience more exuberance than we did in 2016 when LeBron James and the Cavaliers came back from a 3-1 deficit against what could've been labeled the greatest NBA team of all time.

Mike adds: I agree with Jay about Ohio teams challenging the patience of their fan bases with one huge exemption. I went to The Ohio State University where I got to experience championships and great teams and many national championships. However, the Cavs comeback in 2016 was one of the greatest in sports history. Kyrie was amazing, LeBron was amazing, and the entire team was amazing. In

2015, the Cavs came up a little short but that NBA Finals was one of the most impressive series I've ever watched. LeBron was as good as any athlete could be. He was driven with the goal of bringing a championship to Cleveland. Every ounce of his will and ability went into that goal. It was impressive. If the top athletes in any sport gave that much of themselves to a goal, then professional sports would be in far better shape.

> **Jay returns:** Yes, who could forget THE Ohio State University?! Okay, so maybe Mike got spoiled a bit with the seemingly annual Buckeye success, but I think he would agree that we went through our share of character building stress watching our professional sports teams. As a Cleveland Cavaliers fan, I, like so many other loyal Cavs fans, have an ever present hatred for Steph Curry. Now, Steph may very well be the best shooter of all time, but he broke our hearts a few times, let's be honest. I mean thank goodness for 2016 (when the Warriors held the best record in the history of the NBA and were a game away from beating the Cavs in the NBA Finals) when LeBron and our Cavs came back to win an incredible series, one of the greatest comebacks in the history of sports. After the game LeBron exclaimed: "CLEVELAND! THIS IS FOR YOU!!" It was a game seven win that brought so many Cavs fans, including my own father, to tears. And in all honesty, if we wouldn't have won that one, I'm not sure I could even look at Steph Curry.
>
> There are many facets of the way Curry carries himself on the court that are annoying to me, but the one that hurts me the most is when he shoots a three and turns his back and starts running down the floor, and then the damn ball still goes in. I mean, what the heck? How does that happen? How does he do that? Some will watch that shot and say that Curry knows it's going in because of the way it comes off his hand. They will say that he is so used to the way the ball leaves his hand that when he sees it traveling on a certain initial path, he can already realize the end of that arc will

end up in the bottom of the net. I have another theory. I believe he knows it's going in before he shoots it. I believe he knows it's going in BEFORE it leaves his hand, and this is the concept of the "boom mentality."

I often wondered how many times, at the expense of my team, a player hits clutch shots when their team is down, and the only way for the team to win is if they make not just that shot to draw closer, but then another shot to tie, and then another shot to win. I sometimes had this weird thought while grieving a tough loss that if they would've just missed that first shot, then the game would have been over and my team would've won. Then I would get so mad that instead of missing that first shot, they somehow made all three. How did that happen? Why did that guy have to make all three? That player didn't make three shots in a row the entire game, but at the end of the game, when all he has to do is miss this one, he made all three, and every time one goes in, I can hear Mike Breen yell "BANG!"

Mike chimes in: One of the most amazing comebacks I have ever watched was Reggie Miller scoring eight points in nine seconds during the 1995 NBA playoffs to beat the Knicks. I know it was a small deficit to overcome, but for one player to score that many points in that small amount of time made it truly special. However, I am curious to know how it happened. Did the Knicks just go brain dead? Did the Knicks just get tight? Or did Miller just elevate his game beyond all on the court?

Jay continues: What is so different at the end of the game as opposed to other parts of the game where the player will miss wide-open jumpers? The answer is *the degree of challenge*. A player often performs best when his back is against the wall. It's at that point where the fight or flight choice is made, and the great competitors, of course, choose to fight. When they choose to fight, they recognize the challenge, and they realize either consciously or subconsciously that they are going to have to utilize their full arsenal of mental, emotional, and physical skills. However, at other parts of the game, when the challenge isn't perceived as threatening, a player may be using a much smaller percentage of these overall skills. They may still be playing hard and playing to win, but they aren't pushed/inspired to push themselves to the highest gear possible. When LeBron made what I believe was the most ridiculous game-winning shot ever during the 2018 NBA playoffs against Toronto, he knew that HE needed to make a big shot, and I believe he knew he was going to make the shot when he took the inbounds pass. If that is, indeed, the case, and certain athletes have that power, how did they get it? That is where the boom mentality comes in.

To understand how to achieve this mentality, we first need to understand what exactly it is. Achieving the ability to trigger a superior amount of control of getting oneself to simply EXPECT to be successful comes from the development of two levels of confidence. The first of these is what I like to call *momentary confidence*. This is the type of confidence that is built from short term success. Let's use an example from the basketball court. I have played in a basketball league at the Lifetime clubs now for over 10 years and I often play for *The Hooligans*. That name comes from Harris' Hooligans, the name we affectionately called our tennis campers and tennis fans back in my tennis coaching days at Brown University. Throughout these 10years in the UHoops Lifetime League, every stat has been recorded, and I am currently a 51% shooter from the field, but just a 30% shooter from beyond the arc. If I miss a three or two at the beginning of the game, most of the time, I won't attempt another deep shot. My momentary confidence is not very high. However, if I make a three pointer early in a game, and then make another jumper shortly thereafter, my confidence will boom! I will then expect to make the next jumper, and if that one goes in, then my expectations of making the next one are even more certain. This is a level of short term confidence. I don't believe I am a great jump shooter, but on certain nights, I know that I can get in a good groove, and I can shoot at a higher percentage than my average would suggest.

What I wish I had as a shooter is what I like to call *perpetual confidence*. The definition of the word perpetual is "never ending or changing" or "occurring repeatedly." This is a type of confidence that is deeply rooted in an athlete's soul. It comes from hundreds or even thousands of moments of success. When I look at a guy like Damian Lillard pull up from anywhere on the court and nail threes, it shows me that he simply expects every one of them to go in. What is even more impressive though, is when he can do it under what you think would be tremendous pressure. In 2019, with the Trailblazer's season on the line, Lillard dribbled the ball 40 feet from the basket as the last seconds on the clock ticked away, and then pulled up from VERY deep to nail a series ending shot and send Paul George and the Oklahoma City Thunder home. George immediately called this shot a bad shot, but was it? Was it a bad shot, or did Lillard KNOW he would make it? Another question is WHY would Lillard take a shot from that far out with the entire series hanging in the balance? All of his teammates were of course depending on him to make a good choice there as were all of the Portland fans. He made that choice and then proceeded in making the huge shot because he had an extreme level of perpetual confidence. He clearly expected himself to make it, and make it he did!

Mike chimes in: I don't really know where to start in discussing Jay's basketball ability. He is a terrible shooter, he is not a good ball handler, and he is not particularly fast. However, he hustles and gets after it as much as any player that I've ever played with. I can understand why Jay's confidence is a little low when it comes to shooting because he doesn't have great success over a long period of time. In another section of the book we talk about trying to get a basketball player confident early and there's several ways to do this. One way is to keep shooting if you've missed some shots early. However, I'm not a big fan of that method because missed shots are the equivalent of turnovers and both only hurt the team.

Over the years I've given Jay a hard time about this basketball league he plays in because it keeps stats. The only stat that is important to me is wins and losses. However, as a basketball coach, I know that there is an importance to stat lines. Stat lines often determine the wins and losses. Whereas Jay is not a good shooter or a good ball handler, he is a great rebounder because he just keeps getting after and after it, and that is his strength. A player has to know their strengths and you have to bring those every single game to help your team win. If Jay takes a night off from rebounding and hustling, then his team probably is going to lose. Why is Jay a good rebounder? Is it because he's confident in his ability to rebound? Is it his desire to get W's? These are questions that Jay has to answer.

Jay and I recently got back from a little golf trip to Nashville, Tennessee. The first two days of playing I really struggled with my short game. More specifically, my chipping and pitching was atrocious. Typically, I'm pretty confident with all those types of shots but for some reason when I stood over the ball I had zero confidence. I almost just wanted to grab my putter even when I was 20 yards off the green because I had no control of my wedge game. Then on day three about halfway through the round I decided I had enough of this woe is me attitude. So on my next chip shot I didn't think about how I hope this gets on the green or I hope I don't blade it over into the bunker. Instead, I picked a very specific spot on the green where I wanted the ball to land and I focused solely on that spot and nothing else. I'm sure I was having mechanical problems but I needed to first get my mind correct. I got my mind correct by narrowing my focus from the overall large green to a very specific spot. Now what really helped my confidence is I actually hit the spot and hit a good chip shot and just like that my confidence had changed and I was able to play much better finishing out the golf trip.

Jay saunters back into the convo: A terrible shooter? Come on mannnn... That may be the most incredulous comment in this book! Now, one could claim self-bias here, but I would classify myself as a pretty good shooter actually; I'm not great, but pretty good, and I'll make sure to show Mike my stats the next time we are together!

I do want to pick up on Mike's experience around the greens though, as that relates directly to the *Boom Mentality*." When any athlete produces images of what bad things *could* happen (as Mike described he was doing with his wedges), they are bound to produce poor results. On the other hand, when they create positive images, they are giving themselves a chance to produce great results. The positive images correlate directly with positive expectations, and when an athlete can truly believe in an expectation, that allows for a bit of magic to happen, and BOOM, the ball goes in the hole!

So, how do coaches create this magic? Well, the first step is really to build an athlete's ability to create clear and detailed images, and then of course these produced images need to be ones related to almost perfect results. For Mike with his wedge, it was as simple as seeing the picture of hitting the ball to the exact spot on the green. The word *exact* is key here! For my tennis players, it is often visualizing themselves hitting the ball with super smooth mechanics, having the ball land on a specific spot in the court, and then seeing the ball explode by their opponent.

The next step is to create a trigger for the image, and for me, *BOOM* is the word used as a trigger in training sessions. Here is how: I create a goal for the session first. For example, one of my favorite students to work on *Boom Mentality* with is Madison Lee, and we often work on finishing points with her forehand. We aren't yet to the Steph Curry *boom* level yet, but we are getting there! I set up a drill that puts Madison in a position where she needs to execute a very aggressive forehand and as we work on it, I force her to say *BOOM* after every great forehand. This mentally attaches the word *boom* to an image of a perfectly struck forehand. We do this over and over until I feel like it has stuck, and then we change the order. At this point, we continue the same drill, but I make Madison softly say *boom* BEFORE hitting the shot. This forces Madison to create the image before the shot while further attaching boom to the perfect image, and essentially creating an expectation for success. This is also done in repetition until Madison feels she can clearly see the perfect forehand before hitting the shot and importantly, when she believes that the picture is the thing causing the positive result. After this mental training, we put it to the test. Madison is then put into game-like scenarios where the task is to anticipate the opportunity to finish the point with her forehand (it can be called the *boom opportunity*) by producing a pattern in a point that will lead her there. At first, we use the *boom* after capitalizing on the opportunity as a bit of a celebration, and then we reverse the order in the same way we did during the drilling section, where Madison says *boom* as she recognizes her *boom opportunity*, creates the image of hitting the perfect ball, and then cracks a forehand that creates a BOOM heard all across the tennis facility!

As said on most shampoo bottles, "rinse and repeat," and this is critical here. Repetition is so important in building technique, and while many athletes and coaches understand this to clearly be true, they often only realize its role in physical techniques such as stroke mechanics in golf and tennis. Many athletes and coaches make the mistake of believing that a mental technique can be something that once introduced, just sticks in an athlete's brain forever. That is simply not how things go though. If an athlete wants to be elite, mental repetition is vital, and I personally believe the *Boom Mentality* is a great place to start.

Mike finishes: Jay and his stats. Jay is an above average shooter if he has 10 seconds to get the shot off. Watching Jay shoot is like watching the Tin Man shoot.

Jay gets the last word: An upgrade from terrible to above average? Thanks!! Bottom line - 21 championships in 11 years - as Mike says, winning is what is most important. Insert mic drop here...

Mike hands Jay the mic: You are 100% correct, the win column is the most important stat. Shaq has four rings (in a real basketball league, not the Long Island over 50 rec league). Would you call him a good shooter? And I said above average if you have 10 seconds to shoot. Jay is a good example of how important fire is to winning.

Jay has the mic now? Thanks for the compliment? I think...ha

FIRE VERSUS ANGER

I grew up with a father who had the shortest fuse on the planet. I watched him wreck so many good things with his temper. Do not get angry; get fired up.

—Michael Kathrein

I know Jay likes to use "fence it" and I prefer "clean it," mostly because there aren't too many fences close by on a golf course. The reason it is important to "fence it" is to cool the anger. There are very few sports that require anger to be good. I didn't want to say no sport because I am sure someone would try to prove me wrong. Anger is blinding; anger is difficult to control, and anger leads to loss. Fire or drive leads to victory. A player's fire has the potential to put them in a flow state. No such luck when a player goes nuclear.

    I grew up with a father who had the shortest fuse on the planet. I watched him wreck so many good things with his temper. There are so many stories to tell but I will stick to the golf stories. I was in college at the time but was home for the summer. This was the summer that my dad had decided to quit drinking. He suffered from addiction his entire adult life and cost him two marriages, but he decided to make some changes. I am not sure golf is a good sport for someone who recently stopped drinking and spent several days in the hospital suffering from DTs. Golf is a mentally taxing sport and it can frustrate anyone. Taking my short-tempered Dad who was trying to live life sober had the potential to go nuclear, and it did.

    We went to a golf course about four miles from his house or a 20-minute walk as the crow flies. Neither my dad nor I had done much golfing at this time so there should have been no expectations of greatness, but that was not the mindset my dad had on this endeavor.

He thought he was going to par every hole. It is important to know that we were each using 30-year old clubs. The first hole seemed to go fine. He didn't par it. Instead he had an eight. There was no anger at this time, just a chuckle and on to the next tee. Hole number two was a 130-yard par three with a pond just off to the right of the tee box. The pond really wasn't in play on this hole. My Dad teed up the ball, took a few practice swings (he held the club like a baseball bat), took a little waggle, and then finally made his swing. Shank!! The ball went right into the pond! He immediately went absolutely nuclear. The string of curse words that came out of his mouth was actually impressive. My dad was a prolific potty mouth on most days, but he brought his "A" game on this particular day! As the words exploded out, he then suddenly picked up his bag, walked towards the pond and then the guy threw his clubs directly into the water! As the clubs sank, he turned to me and said "drive yourself home," and he proceeded to walk off the golf course.

In his state of mind, my Dad had no control over his actions. He didn't think about the consequences of what he was doing. He was so enraged that he stopped being an athlete and became a maniac. I have seen too many athletes do similar things ...well, not similar, but at least demonstrating an equal lack of control.

> **Jay bursts in:** Wow Mike, that is a fiery start to this chapter indeed! We've referenced a master of the tirade in a previous chapter, and now Mike has provided an example of the disastrous effects that can be caused when an athlete allows anger to control reactions. This makes me think of the great Mike Tyson quote in one of my favorite movies, *The Hangover*: "We all do dumb shit when we get f'ed up." Throwing a golf bag into a pond wasn't the smartest move, but it is also not an entirely unique one.
>
> Not that this is the same level at all, but I had a few moments that served as wake-up calls for me in regards to controlling my own anger. One was in the summer of 1991 when my mom grounded me at the age of 19 after acting like a complete ass

during the mixed doubles finals in my favorite tennis tournament, the Mansfield News Journal. However, my favorite and most attention-getting situation happened a few years earlier. I was playing a practice doubles set against my dad and my other coach, Ron Schaub. My partner, Tucker (referenced earlier as one of the "cool kids") was playing like crap so I had to essentially carry the team to have a shot to win. At the age of 15, I was sort of done losing to my dad and I greatly enjoyed the chance to beat Ron. It was tight though. We were down 2-1 in the first set breaker when Ron hit one of his patented high lobs. Tucker gave no effort to track it down, so it was on me. As I ran back, the damn ball came down and actually hit me, ending the point, and making my blood boil! I slammed my racquet to the clay court and I heard a SNAP. Up to that point, I had never broken a tennis racquet. I had seen countless other players do it, including my idol at the time, John McEnroe, but this was a first for me. I examined the frame and noticed the crack. I slowly walked up to the bench on the side of the court in an effort to switch to my backup racquet. However, my dad intercepted me in that area and told me that I wasn't going to use my other racquet. So, scared to death, I continued with the broken one, and we did not win another point. After the set, my dad had to take me to cross country practice (NOT my favorite thing to do!). On the 12-minute car ride, not a word was spoken. Rarely had my dad ever been speechless when angry, but this was next level for him. Upon arrival at the practice course, I opened the door and stepped out of the car. That's when my dad finally spoke up and he said: "I hope you like this sport." That was a rough cross country practice that day. It was bad enough to just have to randomly run mile after mile in some field, but to do it wondering if my dad would ever let me play tennis again was mortifying.

Ironically, a month ago I had a similar episode with my own fiery son, Mason. He was in a practice that I was helping to coach, and towards the end, as he maybe got a bit physically tired, he also started to express his frustrations. After a few small outbursts,

I told him to settle down. Two minutes later, he lost a point, slammed his racquet against his foot, and that same SNAP was heard by all. The kid broke his racquet on his foot! I was livid!! The practice ended soon after, and as Mason attempted to get into my car, I said: "No, you can ride with your brother." My oldest son Jackson, Mason and I were to drive up to ski for the weekend in Vermont. We drove for two hours in separate cars as I had no interest in hearing from Mason. I of course realized the irony of my own moment with my dad, and I wanted to make sure that Mason learned an equally impactful lesson. So, after we arrived in Vermont at our hotel, and I had cooled off, Mason and I had a very good talk. I wanted to first make sure he understood the ramifications of his actions. I wanted him to realize that a kid who breaks a $200 racquet that was given to him is essentially acting like an entitled spoiled brat showing no appreciation for the materials he has. He got that. But most importantly, I wanted him to learn that he was going to have to build skills to diffuse his own anger. I wasn't telling him that he shouldn't be angry here. I don't follow the "an athlete always has to be positive" methodology. I actually wanted him to learn to feel the anger, identify it, and then find a constructive way to handle it. Mason admitted that he had developed the "habit" of slamming his racquet on his foot even at the smallest sense of anger. We agreed that it was safe to say that this would no longer be an acceptable reaction. Now we needed work to build a different, less destructive, "habit."

Mike adds: I like the parenting techniques but how does a coach handle the tantrums? The throwing of clubs and racquets, the slamming of balls, and vocal outbursts are a sad part of competition. The worst thing a coach can do is to ignore the behavior. Coaches need to take action. There is no one size fits all approach because every athlete is different. A coach needs to take the anger and turn it into fire. Anger is destructive and fire can lead to success.

When a player has an outburst, I immediately approach them. I don't approach with anger because anger breeds anger. I approach calmly and simply ask what is going on with the player. I have received many different answers. In fact, their responses aren't that important. I want the player to talk about the frustration, but not lose all of the passion. Anger is a passion, but not a positive passion. The next step is to stoke the fire. I then redirect the player to a positive action like a great shot they hit earlier in the round or maybe the day before. I want them to think about a positive moment but let the fire from the negative experience fuel their desire to be awesome. Occasionally, a player's outburst is too severe for this action. Only once in my coaching career have I had to remove a player from competition. When you helicopter a club 50 yards in front of many spectators, a coach needs to set an example of acceptable behavior.

> **Jay adds:** A helicopter coach may be the most likely to see a helicopter club or racquet!
>
> I like how Mike brings up the important responsibility of the coach's reaction here, as I agree, that reaction can fuel a bigger outburst; it can create a feeling of shame, OR it can "stoke the fire" as Mike said. This can require some delicate handling at times, and both Mike and I have seen coaches butcher these opportunities. In my opinion, the key factor here relates strongly to the coach-player relationship. Most coaches make the mistake of attempting to treat each player the same, and especially when it comes to intense emotions, that mistake can result in disaster if the coaching technique doesn't match well with the player's personality. For example, if a player comes to a team or an environment with insecurities about things like where they fit in on the team or if they've had enough experience or if they are talented enough to belong, then they will likely need a very positive approach, much like the imagery of a successful moment example Mike just used. This player will need to be talked down a bit from emotions before building the fire back up. I agree that it is important to make

sure the spark doesn't disappear, but it is equally important to show the player that they are supported and believed in. A coach may need to be the one to remind the player of the past positive moments instead of pushing the player to remember the moments themselves, and then work to rebuild the emotions to attach the fire to create a very successful performance.

On the other hand, when a player is more confident (whether rightfully so or not), a different approach can be more effective. I personally LOVE Mike's quote: "Let the fire from the negative experience fuel their desire to be awesome." I love it so much that I had to make sure it exists in this book twice! When a player is confident in themselves, and they become frustrated, that is where the coach can step in and push the player immediately towards a passionate response. I think of my former Brown University player, Adil Shamasdin (Wimbledon quarterfinalist AND has a win over Novak Djokovic), who was an extremely emotional yet very confident guy. He was one of the toughest yet easiest guys for me to coach, and yes, I know that sounds strange. Adil was so tough on himself yet so driven. He expected great performances from himself, from his teammates, and from me! He made me a better coach, which is one of the greatest gifts a player can give, and once he and I both understood the extreme level of competitiveness we both held, pushing each other's buttons became pretty easy on both sides. I could walk on the court and quickly describe in great color how soft he was acting on the court, and he would (as Mike described) turn his frustration for me into an incredible desire to be awesome. He could do it to me too. Adil would test me during practice. If he didn't feel that I was pushing the team hard enough, or the right way, and especially if he saw that I was frustrated, he would throw a strategic jab my way. "Coach! I guess we are just letting these guys do whatever they want today, eh?" Yes, Adil is from Canada, so he definitely used the term "eh." There was no easier way to get under my skin than to accuse me of being inattentive to poor work ethic! Adil of course knew this and he used it to push me to coach to my best ability each day. He knew this would be good for the TEAM, and he of course deep down knew it would be good for his own development.

Mike concludes: Countless times I have watched players turn minor occurrences into anger. Clay surfaces can provide some interesting bounces for tennis players. I was watching Jay play a match decades ago. His opponent caught a bad break because Jay hit a shot that landed on tape and the ball just skidded going underneath the racquet of his opponent. This player threw a major tirade that concluded with him smashing his racquet on the tape. On the next point he swung so hard the ball sailed into the fence behind Jay. It was hard not to laugh, and I probably did laugh. I laughed because I knew the match was over. This guy was done. I knew he didn't have fire, just anger. Jay won that semifinal match and moved onto the finals later that day. What makes a player so angry? I don't always know, but I do know that it is destructive. Instead of allowing destructive behavior, players (and coaches!) should look to produce constructive behavior.

In golf, there are many opportunities for some bad breaks, and that is all they are, bad breaks. Players should not turn a bad break into anger; they need to turn it into fire. My team was playing in the District tournament at Sycamore Springs Golf Course, in Arlington, Ohio. On the fourth hole there was a tree really close to the fairway and if a player pushed their tee shot just a little there was a good chance that it would hit the tree. The first two players in the group I was watching hit the tree but the ball bounced back to the left and into the fairway. My number one player, Alex Sazdanoff, was the next to play and she hit this tree. I was standing next to the tee box and watched the ball strike the tree and kick pretty far to the right and into a trouble area. Alex's response was not the best. She said, "Stupid tree, of course it kicked my ball to the right; everyone else got lucky, why didn't I?" Alex and I had a talk as we walked to her ball. The first thing I pointed out was that she hit a tree. I asked Alex if she was trying to hit the tree and have it bounce into the fairway. Alex said, "No." I then pointed out that if you don't hit good shots, then don't expect good breaks. We then discussed her swing and getting her focused back on her positive shots. The last thing I said to Alex was to use the failure of the tee shot to get focused on hitting a good recovery shot to get back into the hole.

Getting back to Jay and his finals match from decades ago. Jay lost the first set and he had a lot of dialogue going at this point. Then, in the first game of the second set, Jay's opponent hit a shot that hit the edge of the center line and the ball kicked away from Jay. At this point, Jay had a mini tirade. At least to most observers it seemed to be a tirade. However, it wasn't an actual tirade, it was constructive self-talk that would turn into fire. At the conclusion of his mini tirade, Jay said something very important. He said, "You're not going to lose like this." He had realized that he was playing with some negative energy. So, before his opponent made his next serve, Jay said (aloud of course), "Let's go." Then he went up on his toes and stepped side to side, releasing the tension in his body. Jay won in three sets.

PART TWO: POWER OF SPORTS

After sports experiences molded and shaped who we were as kids, unique paths seemed to be created in front of us. On our personal journeys, a love for helping athletes be positively impacted in all sorts of TEAM environments grew, and we, as coaches on courts, courses, fields and classrooms, knew that meaningful encounters with the highs and lows of competitions would create values that would last for LIFE.

Here in GAME SET LIFE, we will provide a clear roadmap to success, sharing the specific tools and strategies we've used in navigating our own crusade to find the true Power of Sports. While the obvious goal in sports is to produce wins, the most important goals center around the process in creating successful moments. Dealing with adversity is of course a huge part of this process, and the most mentally strong athletes have an ability to coach themselves through constructive self-talk and visual imagery in order to "clear the mechanism".

The result of the learned skills will not only create better athletes, but also athletes with strengths that are highly sought out by future employers. For example, college athletes often have a desire to perform at the highest levels and to be clutch in doing so. Their "never give up attitude" also adds to the lore, while their ability to understand the importance of even the littlest of choices helps build the grit and character that define true athletes. This is why companies come to colleges to specifically recruit athletes!

We are excited to share the second section of our book with readers who believe in the Power of Sports and want to feel that power on a daily basis.

SETTING GOALS

> *Any athlete worth a lick will set goals every practice and every game. Goals are challenges. Challenges are the root of competition.*
>
> —Michael Kathrein

Every season I ask my captain to set two team goals and I ask each player to set one personal performance goal. The criteria are basic; the goal must be challenging and realistic. I have found that too many players set goals way too high or way too low. Why can't the criteria be met? A player that had an 18-hole average of 110 in 2019 sets a personal goal of an average of under 80. The goal was challenging but not realistic. A thirty stroke drop in a single calendar year is not going to happen often. I appreciate the optimism, but the player is setting themselves up for failure. I had another player who averaged 91 in 2017. She set her 2018 goal to be a bogey golfer. One whole stroke! That goal wasn't challenging. I asked her why she set her goal at improving by just one stroke. Her reply was very disappointing. Her mom said that it would be good to achieve the goal so she could earn the certificate I hand out at the end-of-the-season banquet for those who achieve their goals.

> **Jay quips:** oh my god!! Why do those create "easy goals," otherwise known as "lower expectations?" Well, it's to protect themselves from the disappointment of not meeting an expectation, and parents are so often the first ones working to PROTECT their children in this manner. I would rather my kids set their goals high and achieve half of them than set them low and achieve all of them. Is that just me? I hope not, because I believe wholeheartedly

that is a key to equipping an athlete and/or student with a high level of achievement motivation!

Mike continues: An 'interestingly humorous' example of successful goal setting was done by Ella in 2016:

The team and I were on our way to a tournament at White Pines Golf Club, in Swanton, Ohio. We left Lexington High School around 5:30 a.m. in hopes to arrive by 7:30, and we stopped to get a little breakfast at a McDonalds on the way. As we pulled into the parking lot, I told the girls to order wisely because there wasn't a bathroom along the remaining route to the golf course, which was still about 40 minutes away. They didn't listen well, but Ella assured me that they would all make it.

As we motored down the road, the girls finished off their McMuffins and sugary coffee nightmares. We were smack in the middle of farm country without a gas station on the horizon when I checked the rear view mirror and noticed Ella. She seemed to be in some discomfort and once we locked eyes, she subtly informed me that she had to go to the bathroom. I reiterated to her that there wasn't a place to stop and it was going to be 20 minutes before we got to the golf course. This information did not suit her. A few minutes later I again looked in the mirror and made eye contact with. She quickly said, "I'm scared, coach" and then two more players chimed in to report their bathroom hopes. I offered to pull into the driveway of a farmhouse along the way, but that was rejected quickly. Our van continued along and the team was definitely becoming increasingly agitated as every minute passed. They were screaming at me to drive faster, but every little bump in the road created a trauma. Finally, we turned a corner and saw the golf course on the horizon. The girls all unbuckled their seatbelts and were on the edge of their seats ready to bolt out of the van. They all made it! At McDonalds, Ella set a goal to have her coffee and not have to use the restroom before the golf course. It was definitely a goal that met the criteria of being challenging and realistic!

Jay's turn: You can read about more "bathroom adventures" in my future book *"THE REAL COLLEGE ATHLETES, The College Tour the Guides Never Took You On,"* but those are a little different than this one! Haha

But okay, back to the goals: Mike brings up the most important aspects in the foundation of goal-setting. Setting goals that are realistic but challenging can seem simple, but many times it is not. There are a lot of influencers around making impacts on the goals, and it is near impossible to have everyone's expectations match in terms of what is and is not realistic and challenging.

So, what does the goal-setter do? Who does he/she listen to when setting his/her goals? Mike, you tell a great story here with the mother who wants her daughter to be successful. That mother has probably heard the cliché', "shoot for the stars, expect to be shot down." Is that a cliché' or did I just make that up?

Mike takes a swing: I haven't heard that one but that doesn't mean it isn't a cliché. There is nothing wrong with a cliché because they are based on self-evident truths. Of course there is a strong chance of getting shot down when you shoot for the stars. Here is where I point out the obvious: we learn more from our failures than our successes; goals are very important for growth. I like to set a strong goal and work toward achieving that goal. If I come up a little short of achieving that particular goal, did I fail? I don't think so. First, I worked hard. That is a win. Second, I probably improved at least one skill. That is another win. Third, I will reflect on why I fell short of my goal (hence learn). That is a win as well. In one failed goal I could get three wins.

Jay comes back: I really like the concept of the "three wins." Goals are about setting up expectations for upcoming performances AND about learning from what happens in regards to those set goals. This leads me to discuss some specific guidelines when making goals.

My buddy, Danny Pellerito, and I had many off-court mental-work sessions to build strong mental skills and also to prepare for certain tennis tournaments. At the end of each session, we would always set specific goals for the upcoming tournament, and I would of course coach Danny on how exactly to create the most helpful goals possible. When doing this, we would keep in mind some simple guidelines.

The first of these was to understand the importance of making goals "measurable." If an athlete (or a student or just a person!) creates a number of goals that are not measurable, then how can he/she truly know how well they performed against the goal? Many players will create goals such as "I want to play to the best of my ability" or "I want to display a good attitude." Now, those goals are good actually; however, it is very hard to measure them. When Danny and I would set up his goals for each tournament, we would always set three goals. My simple rule for him was that two of the three would have to be truly measurable. This helped us greatly evaluate how he was progressing at each turn. These goals were sometimes as general as "I want to win the tournament" but often much more specific and detailed like "I want my first serve percentage to be above 70%" or "I want to break serve in one of my opponent's first three service games of each set."

I wanted Danny to create goals that were challenging for sure (as Mike referenced), but also those that led him to achieving what we felt he needed to in order to progress his overall game. An example of a set of goals showing this surrounded our insistence that Danny play a more aggressive game style. Danny was an extremely consistent player, but as his level (and that of his opponents') increased, he would need to become a more assertive player. He couldn't just rely on his opponent missing as much. He would need to TAKE more points. Thus, our specific goals would reference that. Danny was usually one of the shorter players on the court, and a shorter tennis player is often expected to have a weaker serve. I worked to create the opposite mentality for Danny as I wanted him to believe that his serve was a big weapon. We of course worked on his serve technique to create a powerful motion, but that wasn't going to be enough, especially in the heat of battle. Danny would need to truly BELIEVE that his serve was big, and that his serve could win him big points. So, a lot of our goals during this mind-set production would center around winning points with the serve. One common one was a goal I borrowed from Ty Tucker, head men's coach at the Ohio State University. He would tell his players that they must win two "free points" with their serve every service game. A "free point" is one where a player hits a serve big enough or placed well enough that the opponent can either not return it, or returns it weak enough for an easy put-away. For Danny, when we started using this as a goal, he was lucky to win two free points per match with his serve! Danny's match goals started to include things like "I want to win one free point per game" or "I want to win one BIG point at the end of a game with my serve each set" and then progressed to "I want to win two free points per game" and "I want to finish three games per match with a service winner/ace." These goals created a completely different mind-set for Danny and it is something that he carried with him throughout his junior and college career!

Notice that I did say two of three goals needed to be measurable. I did allow for one of those three goals to be tougher to calculate. Interestingly, this third goal became a constant one for Danny. While creating measurable goals is extremely important, the immeasurable goals can also be. For Danny, his most common immeasurable goal was this: "I want to work harder than every opponent I play." While that goal was almost impossible to truly assess, it may have been the most important of his goals because it helped him create a true on-court identity. My point is this: when building goals, create measurable ones, and when creating those tougher to measure, make sure those are creating a large impact on expectations and/or the overall mind-set.

Another important aspect in building goals is to create goals that are performance-related as opposed to outcome-related. The easiest goals to create are outcome goals. An outcome goal is exactly that - a goal that pertains to the outcome of a performance. The most obvious one is "I want to win the match/game." Other outcome goals were referenced above like "I want to win two free points per game." Outcome goals are not bad at all; however, it is also key to include performance goals as well. For Danny, our "perceived toughness" goals were great performance ones for sure. "I want to make my opponent check out of the match" was one of my favorite ones. Performance goals are often tougher to make measurable, but not impossible. For example, a basketball player could create a goal like, "I want to keep my elbow in on every jump shot" or a golfer could create one like, "I want to judge the speed well on each of my putts in the upcoming round." Both of these goals focus on physical performance and mental strategy and even a little on emotional control (the three most important performance aspects), but are also measurable. A basketball player can go back and watch the tape with his/her coach or parent and keep stats on how many jump shots were made with the proper technique. A golfer can measure the distance of every second putt during a round. These are great performance goals that are also measurable.

Mike concludes: Performance goals are the key to good goal setting. When a player enters a tournament his/her goal is to win the tournament. Well, guess what? Every player in the field has that goal. So, we have to break down an 18-hole event into smaller performance-based goals. I know in basketball and football, many coaches talk about winning each quarter. Or maybe the first four minutes of a half. That is breaking it down into smaller goals, but are they really performance-based? In golf, when players are standing on the first tee they are typically thinking about hitting the fairway with the first shot. "Okay, let's just get something in play" is a common thought on the first tee. Yes, this is a goal but how will the player achieve that goal? A common mishap on the first tee is to get a little anxious with the swing and slide in front of the ball, usually causing a low draw or hook. And yes the ball is in play but the ball is in the left rough or behind a tree or in a penalty area. A good performance-based goal for the first tee is to keep your head behind the ball.

Jay chimes in: I need to remember that!!

Mike continues concluding: The player on the first tee sets the first goal of the round and that is to keep his/her head behind the ball. That should be a goal on all shots, but the verbalization or inner dialogue will create the goal. To have a good round of golf and compete to win, a player must set many performance goals. A good example of a performance-based goal is to hit 14 of 18 greens in regulation. Another good example in a round of golf is having 32 putts or less for the round. How can players limit the number of putts? Set a performance goal of keeping everything still and just using their shoulders to putt. Golf is an easy game to set performance goals because there are so many variables and measurable components of the game, and one round typically lasts four hours. Most athletic competitions are much shorter in time and players need to focus on just one or two performance goals. No matter what the competition is, a successful player will often be the one that can break the competition into small parts and create performance-based goals.

LIFE CHOICES

One can go out and actively smell the roses, OR they can sit back and wait for the smell of the roses to be seen. It is tough to see the smell in my opinion.

Little choices aren't so little!

—Jay Harris

I was the head men's tennis coach at Bowling Green State University when email became sort of a thing. Yes, I am old. Email wasn't always around; believe it or not. The internet wasn't either. Ok, I digress. I remember that email inbox getting flooded a bit with some spam from time to time, and while most of it was highly deletable (is that a word? I think maybe it is now!), there was one spam email story that stood out to me. It was the story of Ben and Mark.

Ben and Mark were new high school students who weren't much more than acquaintances where this story picks up. Mark, who had just recently moved into town, was a small freshman who seemed to be constantly picked on by peers. Ben was also a freshman, and while he was aware that Mark had been having his struggles with certain bullies, he hadn't seen anything like what he saw on this certain Wednesday. Mark was walking home after school across the same field he always traveled through when a group of kids approached him from behind and proceeded to knock him over. They then opened his backpack and threw all of the contents of the pack into the grass. This was a bit of a hit and run as the bullies took off after the knockdown, but the damage was done. Mark was crying intensely as he tried to collect all of the papers that were blowing all over the field and put them back into the trapper keeper that was in his backpack, along with the scientific calculator (yes it still worked) and all of the #2 pencils that were scattered all over. That moment was when Ben made his first important choice. He saw the attack happen and immediately ran over to Mark to help him collect his belongings. Once collected, Ben had another choice to make. Now, Mark's home was about a mile east of the school while Ben lived west of the school. He could have of course said goodbye to Mark after helping him, but instead, he chose to walk with him all the way to his house as Mark still seemed very upset after the attack. Not much was said on that walk, but Ben felt good about the choice he made to escort Mark home. Once arriving at Mark's house, Ben noticed that it seemed as if no one was home. That's when he made a third important choice. He chose to stay with Mark at his house until his parents arrived home. Ben and Mark became best friends and Mark turned out to be a brilliant student. In fact, he became the valedictorian of his class. It was at graduation where the true importance of Ben's choices on that Wednesday was brought to light. Mark shared with the class of graduates how tough his first few months in this town and school were for him. He shared how depressed he became during this time and how a couple of choices completely changed the course of his life. You see, Mark had a plan on that Wednesday. He knew that his parents would not be home when he would arrive after school, and his plan was to walk home and kill himself that day. Obviously Ben's choices completely changed that plan and subsequently, the path of his life.

Now, I don't know about your reaction to hearing that story, but to this day, every time I tell it, I get chills. That story more than any became a blueprint for me to cry out about the importance of little choices one is faced with in life, and how impactful these choices can be! And not surprisingly, I began to realize the amazing impacts of little choices that were happening all around me! Here is one of them:

As the head men's tennis coach at Brown University from 2002-2010, we had many simple rules. One of those rules was to walk around with your head up. Now that may seem like a strange rule to some, but it was something I found important when I moved to the east coast. I grew up in Ohio and never really noticed this so much, but most people when they would walk around town would say hello when they passed you, and for me, most would ask me if I was Chriss Harris's son (I got annoyed by that as a kid, but grew to realize that I should be proud of my incredibly successful mom!). When I moved to Rhode Island and the east coast, I immediately noticed that almost everyone walked around with their head down. Other than my very outgoing first assistant coach, Matt Shaine, who said hello to EVERYONE, no one really even spoke to each other when passing on the street. There were times that I would say hello and the response was almost of shock. I would get this look like "why are you talking to me" or "what the hell do you want?" Now, I think only a couple of passers-by actually said those things out loud to me, but it was a huge change from what I was used to in Ohio. So, I wanted my Brown University tennis team to reflect more of the values I was brought up with as opposed to what was going on in the east, and that is where the rule, "walk with your head up" came about. Richard Moss was a very talented player on our team, and he was from South Africa. Richard, along with his teammates, had heard me speak of the head up rule many times, and on one fateful day, HE experienced its importance. Richard had to leave practice just a touch early on this day as he needed to rush across campus to attend a symposium of sorts regarding his major, architecture. Richard was rushing to the lecture hall and because he was keeping his head up, he noticed a man who was obviously lost. Richard had a choice to make. He could either help the man, or he could continue to rush to the event in an attempt not to be late. Richard went up to the man asking where he was going, and the response was ironic. The man was going to the same event that Richard was doing his best to attend. So, Richard escorted him to the hall. On the way, this man sort of announced that it was embarrassing that he was going to be late, because HE was the lead speaker of the symposium! One can imagine that Richard's head popped up even higher after hearing that! They traveled to the event together, and upon arrival, the man asked Richard to sit in the front row. After the speech, Richard went up to show his appreciation along with the admiration of the work this famous architect had been involved with. The appreciation was shared right back to Richard, and in fact, that next summer, Richard was the only underclassman asked to serve as an intern in this incredible architectural firm. Even more amazing than that, is that just a year later, this same firm was asked to be the lead consultants in the World Trade Center Memorial in New York City, and Richard was able to be along for the ride, all because he kept his head up while walking across campus!

In my many years of sport psychology consulting, I have told those two stories many times, but I have also brought the choices to a more specific arena, the actual court. This could be a basketball court, tennis court, football field or whatever, where the importance of little choices a competitor is faced with making cannot be over-exaggerated in my opinion. To explain the process in making certain choices, I often break it down with an example regarding the obstacle of handling stress or possibly some troubling circumstances. For instance, let's say a tennis player has missed a shot on the court on a huge point that could end up determining the outcome of the match. That player has three choices. He can let it bother him (that is the easiest choice and the one most commonly made!). He can "deal with it" – this is usually a tougher choice and one requiring a certain skill set. Or, he can "fence it."

To explain the "fence it" choice, I will have to go back to my days at Miami of Ohio where I was once reading a book by sport psychologist, Terry Orlick. Dr. Orlick told a story about an expedition he once made to do some research on the sporting behaviors of certain tribes in New Guinea. While monitoring the play methods of the tribal members, Dr. Orlick noticed one particular interesting act that they all made. The sporting events that were played amongst the tribesmen were often very aggressive, and at the completion of each session of games, all of the men would line up in front of a certain tree, and one by one would approach the tree, touch it, and then return to their homes. Dr. Orlick of course was very curious about this and asked the chief of the tribe to explain why that was happening. The chief told him that the men all lined up in front of the tree in order to release all of their aggressive energy into the tree before returning to their homes. The tribe did not want the aggressiveness of the games to return with them to their home lives, so the tree provided a very important dumping ground for any negativity. Dr. Orlick found this fascinating and brought it back to Canada, where he was working with a group of tennis players at the time. He coached them to use the fence that surrounds the court they were playing on the same way the tribesmen used the tree. If players weren't capable of dealing with any frustration, negativity or even nervousness during a match, they were instructed to go back, touch the fence and visualize any of those bad thoughts leaving their heads, and moving into the fence.

Shortly after reading about this, I became a junior consultant working out of my sport psychology grad program, and my first client was a tennis player (shocking, right?!). Her name was Audra Falk and at the time she was ranked in the top 10 in the nation for girls 12 & under. Audra had already run through a few coaches in her "career" up to that point, and she was dealing with plenty of negative emotional issues on the court, which is why her parents had reached out to my program for help. I saw Audra once a week for about a year and to be honest, when we started, Audra wasn't necessarily happy to see me each week. I was likely destined to be just another in Audra's graveyard of coaches, until we hit a bit of lightning in a bottle. During one of our sessions, I decided to tell Audra the story of the New Guinea tribesman and how that concept could possibly help her on the court. She immediately looked me right in the eye and said, "Jay, that's the dumbest thing I've ever heard in my entire life!" I retreated a bit, absorbing Audra's strike and moved on to the next topic. A week later, I came in to visit with Audra again, and for some strange reason, she was super excited to see me! This had me confused already. Audra and I went into our session room and she immediately began talking as if she had 10 seconds to explain a 10-minute story or else a bomb would blow up her entire house! She was like:

> "JAY! YOU AREN'T GOING TO BELIEVE THIS!! I WOKE UP THIS MORNING AND REALIZED THAT MY MOM FORGOT TO WAKE ME UP! OMG!! SO I GO DOWNSTAIRS AND GET YELLED AT FOR NOT BEING READY YET. LIKE WHAT THE HELL! SO I HAD TO GET READY IN LIKE FOUR MINUTES AND THEN MY DAD TELLS ME THAT THEY ARE TAKING MY DOG TO THE VET TODAY BECAUSE HE IS SICK AND ALSO THAT MY AUNT IS PICKING ME UP AFTER SCHOOL AND I HATE WHEN SHE DOES THAT BECAUSE SHE DOESN'T KNOW HOW TO DRIVE AND SO THEN I GO TO SCHOOL AND REALIZE THAT I LEFT MY HOMEWORK ON MY NIGHT TABLE IN MY ROOM AND THEN THE NEXT CLASS WE HAD A STUPID POP QUIZ WHICH I OF COURSE FAILED AND THEN I WAS FREAKING OUT ABOUT MY DOG BECAUSE I DIDN'T EVEN KNOW WHAT WAS WRONG WITH HIM AND THEN MY AUNT WAS LATE PICKING ME UP FROM SCHOOL AND THEN THAT MADE ME LATE TO PRACTICE SO MY STUPID TENNIS COACH YELLED AT ME AND THEN I GOT ON COURT AND LITERALLY MISSED THE FIRST TEN BALLS I HIT AND THEN STARTED FREAKING OUT BECAUSE I COULDN'T MAKE A FRICKIN' BALL AND THEN I REMEMBERED THAT STUPID THING THAT YOU TOLD ME SO I DECIDED TO TRY IT FOR SOME

UNKNOWN REASON AND I WALKED BACK TO THE FENCE AND TOUCHED IT AND oh my god, I felt amaaaaaaaazing. All of a sudden I was hitting incredibly well and couldn't miss and I literally had the best practice of my entire life! All thanks to you Jay!"

Ok, now maybe I added that last part with the thank you myself, but I think you get the point!

Fencing works but ONLY if the "fencer" believes it will work. I have had many players use this fencing technique and I have had many more make up their OWN technique. The little "tricks" are the alternatives to doing the heavy lifting of dealing with a certain obstacle in the exact moment it appears. One of the tricks that I personally use is my "hat technique." When I compete in a tennis tournament, I always wear a hat. Now, I went through a period in my tennis career where I was quite the hot head. I would get so mad on the court that I was known to break a racquet or two. Racquets were (and are) expensive to replace though, so I turned my frustration towards my hat. I would often be seen throwing tantrums on the court expressing my frustrations pretty openly, and one of my go-to moves was to throw my hat on the ground as hard as I could. I once actually threw a certain hat so many times that I broke the back of the hat and had to toss it in the garbage mid match. I doubt I won that one! In the summer of 1992 I watched a playback of one of my matches that was actually broadcast by a local tv station. I had won the match and the tournament 6-0, 6-4, but I was absolutely embarrassed to see how ridiculous I looked throwing my hat all over the court. What was I doing?! I had been known in the past as a player who showed almost no emotion. I was once told that no one could tell if I was winning or losing when they watched me play. But now I was acting like a buffoon! It was painfully awful to watch, and I immediately changed my attitude. I needed a "trick" though. I was (and still am) an intensely competitive perfectionist, and these frustrations of not performing to a level of my own expectations were not just going to disappear. I needed a place to put them.

So, I turned back to my hat. From that day on, any time I would get frustrated to a point that I couldn't handle it (in other words, on the verge of a tantrum), I would simply take my hat off and I would imagine the steam from my head exiting from the top. When the steam stopped coming out, then I would put my hat back on. Now, if I was really really mad, well then I would go over and put some cold water inside the brim of my hat, and when I put the hat back on my head, I would see the steam produced from my hot head hitting the wet hat brim! And that all worked amazingly well. Why did it work? It worked because I believed in my "trick" and I was willing to make the little choice to turn to that trick every time instead of choosing to let the frustrations bother me and thus, destroy any chance that my performance could be elite.

Mike chimes in: Jay and buffoonery go hand and hand, but he is spot on. At Lexington High School I am the advisor for the school newspaper. Each issue I give out the Cowboy Awards. I periodically pick a couple students who did something in the spirit of John Wayne. Hollywood's interpretation of the cowboy differs from the reality of cowboy life in the 19th century, but Hollywood has a great notion. The Hollywood notion of the cowboy is one of selflessness. This is something I am constantly trying to teach, especially with my athletes. I came up with the Cowboy Awards when I was standing in the hallway between classes. A girl was walking down the hall and she dropped a bottle of water. A boy walking behind her then kicked the bottle away from her and laughed.

At the time I didn't know who that boy was but he quickly learned who I was. I have no tolerance for those who make the choice not to help someone in need. Instead of ranting to all of my students about this boy's misdeeds I chose to highlight the students who help others. It is the little things that matter. The simplest of gestures can have an amazing impact on someone.

Jay responds: That's awesome!

Mike continues: I was born with a hole in my heart and I required a couple of surgeries to repair the birth defect. The first surgery was when I was three months old and it left a good sized scar on my left side just under my arm. The second surgery occurred when I was six years old and left a larger scar right down the middle of my chest. Growing up I was always very self-conscious about my scars particularly the one on my chest. At basketball open gyms we always went shirts and skins. This was a nightmare for me because somehow I was always on the skins team. I was already short and skinny, which magnified my scars.

When I was a freshman at a summer open gym something happened that changed my life. Lexington was hosting the open gym and players from all the area schools were there. One of the best players in the area was a senior from Malabar High School and his nickname was Magic. The teams were chosen and I was a skin of course and Magic was on the other team. I have no idea why he was going to guard me. I was the worst one on my team. We were both guards, but that still doesn't explain why he chose to guard me. As we were getting ready to start, I had the ball under my arm at the top of the key. Just before I was going to check the ball, Magic stepped right in front of me and took the knuckle on his index finger and ran it down my scar making a zipper sound.

That simple gesture changed my life. Magic was just goofing around but it made me realize something about myself. If the scar didn't make someone as popular and cool as Magic uncomfortable, why should I be uncomfortable with it?

I think my players get annoyed with me for constantly talking about the "little things." When a player is in a tournament they have many choices to make on every hole. I'm not just talking about what club to hit or what target to choose. I am also referring to how the player will interact with other players.

When a golfer is playing in a tournament there is at least one other competitor in the playing group, but typically there are two or three players. On many occasions these competitors will be strangers, and during a round, there will be so many opportunities to make a difference in their lives. A player may hit an errant shot into tall grass. He or she may be frustrated, and words of encouragement may go a long way to helping a competitor. Many people might wonder why they should worry about helping a competitor during a tournament. The reason is twofold; the first reason is because a person can. If a player has the ability to help someone he or she should. The second reason is that the good deed will come back to help. Every player will hit a bad shot during a tournament and all should encourage all.

This interaction is a great way to "clean it." Jay uses the phrase "fence it" and I like to use the term "clean it." The principle is the same. When a person is competing, frustrations can build. There has to be a positive outlet for the frustration, or things will get worse and worse. In tennis there can be a lot of racquet throwing, slamming the racquet into the ground or net, smashing the ball into the fence, and many other actions similar to a toddler throwing a temper tantrum. In golf, there is a ton of cursing, slamming the club on the ground and the occasional helicoptering of a club. On the most special occasions there is the entire bag toss. The goal is to "clean it" before it gets to the bag toss into a pond stage of frustration.

The slamming of the club or racquet down isn't entirely futile if done for the right reasons. If that slamming motion gets rid of the frustration, then it was a good reaction. If the player slams the club down and still is frustrated, then it was just the temper tantrum of a toddler. I tell my players to "clean it" in reference to cleaning the golf ball. After a player makes a double bogey or worse on a hole, the player is normally frustrated and will be thinking about everything that was done wrong on the previous hole as he or she is teeing off on the next hole. I don't want this to happen. So, I tell the player to clean the ball. Most holes have ball washers next to the tee box. I want the player to clean the ball to take a moment and just refresh his or her mind. When the ball is getting cleaned it's a fresh start. When the player's hand touches the ball washer he/she is releasing the frustrations. Instead of talking to the player about the double bogey, I just make eye contact with the player and say "clean it."

This is not a full proof plan to get a player focused. The key to "clean it" or "fence it" is belief. In any competition there are negative plays, negative shots, and negative comments. The successful players are the players who can "clean it." Unfortunately, I see more players unable to "clean it." Until five years ago I never discouraged a player from a quick slam of the club after a bad shot. I felt something quick and discreet and not too demonstrative was better than allowing a player to sort of stew in their frustration. However, I changed my approach to this release.

The first reason I changed my approach was that it was a negative reaction to a negative action. This isn't basic multiplication where a negative times a negative equals a positive. Too often the negative reaction just magnified the negative action. So problems were being compounded. I wanted to develop a more positive approach to dealing with negatives during competition. Practice is the right venue to correct the negatives of a competition. The competition needs to stay positive, so I want my players to not dwell on the previous shot or hole.

The second reason I changed my approach was that it just wasn't working. The players I deal with are 15 to 18 years old. They looked at the slamming of the club down as an excuse to magnify the negative. After the next bad shot they slammed the club a little harder, and then a little harder. The players were just unable to let go. They were holding on to the negatives. I adopted the "clean it" method to find a more productive method of releasing frustration. By actually cleaning the ball the player is doing something to prepare for the next hole.

> **Jay adds:** The "clean it" reminds me of my favorite all time movie, *For Love of the Game*. If you haven't seen it, you should! In the movie, Kevin Costner plays an agingß baseball pitcher, Billy Chapel, and as he pitches a game at Yankee Stadium, he finds himself chronicling important moments in his life, moments that made him who he is and brought him to that point in his life. In

one particular scene, Chapel comes to the mound to throw his first pitch and the crowd is going crazy. They are calling him names and being as obnoxious as only a Yankees fan can be. (Sorry, I'm a Red Sox fan so maybe I'm a little biased in judgment!) Chapel stares at the catcher's mitt and simply says "clear the mechanism" and suddenly from his perspective, all of the outside noise fades away. He only sees himself and the catcher. The entire crowd disappeared. It was super cool! Obviously someone with some Sport Psychology knowledge wrote that scene!

QUITTING IS HABITUAL

SO, never quit!

—Unknown

Hall of Fame quarterback Brett Favre's father died of a sudden heart attack in the middle of his 2003 football season. This tragedy actually happened the night before his Packers were to take on the Raiders, but there was seemingly never a doubt that Favre would play in the game. After his incredible performance throwing for 399 yards and four touchdowns that day, he was asked how he got himself to play at all, let alone to that level. Favre replied simply, "I knew my dad would have wanted me to play." Favre's dad cemented this no-quit mentality so deeply into Brett's mind, and one explanation gave a clear representation as to the degree of seriousness this mentality carried. Favre once told reporters that his dad had told him that there was literally only one reason for quitting a game. Mr. Irvin Favre had explained clearly to his son that he was allowed to quit under only once circumstance, and that was when the only way to exit the field of play would be to be carried off. In other words, Favre would be allowed to quit if, and ONLY IF, he couldn't physically get off the field under his own power, and that he would require assistance to leave the field. This sentiment rang true to me, as it was one that was also deeply ingrained into my mentality growing up.

As was referenced in the preface, my dad was a "movie type of coach." My dad's coaching style was a sort of combination of the likes of *Norman Dale - Hoosiers, Herb Brooks - Miracle, Mickey Goldmill - Rocky, and Lou Brown - Major League.* All of these coaches had their "moments." Brooks had his "again" quote; Dale had his insistence on five passes before a shot; Mickey's moment was his exclamation, "get up you SOB," and Brown's best may have been the humorous quip, "Nice catch Hayes. Don't ever f'in' do it again." My dad had many similar "moments," but his most imposing moment came during my freshman year tennis season. As a freshman in high school, I was starting to become an accomplished tournament tennis player, and I was able to make the varsity tennis team. Now, I was actually the 2nd or (at worst) 3rd best player on the team, but because of the coach, I was put into the 2nd doubles position (ranking me 6/7 in the line-up). This "coach" happened to be my dear ole' dad, and he essentially wanted to make it clear to anyone and everyone that he wasn't one to play any favorites. Late in the season, I was given a rare opportunity to play singles (a top 3 position) in the line-up, and at the end of the first set in that match, my dad motioned me to come up to him at the fence. My dad had this way of making me cry just with a certain look, so I of course approached the fence with some grave hesitation. But approach the fence I did. As I got there, my coach/dad started in on his rant. He began his rant: "Jay, not only are you embarrassing yourself out on this court, you are also embarrassing me. I mean hell, you are embarrassing your whole f'ing team, your school, and you are embarrassing your family. Now listen to me. If you don't pick it the f' up, then I am going to rip your ass off the court." I replied, "But Dad, I'm up 5-2!" And my dad quickly replied, "And that is why you will never be a good tennis player!" That was one of my dad's "moments," a moment of very tough love that emulated so many aspects of his coaching. I am sure some would say that was maybe not the best coaching method, and definitely not the most socially correct by today's standards, but he was old school, and he knew how to push buttons psychologically to get the performance out of the kids he coached. He wasn't afraid to get in a player's face whether they were playing well or not, and through experiencing this as a player and a son, I developed a bit of a shell. By the way, I won that match 6-2, 6-0 and only lost three points after that "speech."

My experience with that team was an interesting one for sure. Back in the early 80s, hazing was kind of still allowed, and for our team, freshmen were commonly thrown into showers with all of their clothes on. Mike also made the team and was a bit of a swing player (rotating between varsity and JV), and he was often a target of said hazing.

Mike responds: Jay has an interesting interpretation of events. Maybe his interpretation is accurate but just in case some of the events are allowed to be open for interpretation, here is a different version. I wasn't the target of hazing because I was a swing player. I was a target for hazing because I had an older sister and a friend who wanted to protect himself. Let me first address the swing player nonsense. I consistently was in the sixth spot on a seven-player roster. We had challenge matches where players could challenge for the next spot. The players that were behind me were juniors and classmates of my sister. I beat them every single time, yet the coach kept allowing the challenges. I never got to challenge for the fifth spot because I was always being challenged from the seventh spot. It's tough for a player to grow and advance if they are always looking over their shoulder, right? My goal was not to be six or to be on the varsity team. My goal was to improve and win matches. That is how the team did better. Right before the sectional tournament, the coach allowed another challenge match. This player (who I beat a million times before) got another shot to take my spot right before the biggest tournament to that point. I won 7-4 and started to walk off the court.

The challenger says "where are you going?"
I replied, "It's over, that's seven."
This "great guy" responded: "No it's not, it's five-all."

And of course an argument then commenced culminating with the coach coming down and announcing that it must have been five-all. I wasn't even upset because this nonsense had been going on all year. In fact, I would have been disappointed if the coach said I had won. By the way, I even used math to prove that it was 7-4 and not five-all. One score was an even number and the other an odd number. My challenger agreed that he served the first game and the last game. Apparently, logic was a lost cause. The coach stuck around to verify the rest of the match and I was able to win, and thus, be selected to play in the sectional tournament.

My freshman year was a complete exercise in mental toughness. My high school had a courtyard and the courtyard had a manhole with a loose cover. Upperclassmen liked to stuff freshmen down the manhole.

Jay chimes in: Wait, is that really true? Freshmen got stuffed into a manhole in the courtyard? How did I not know about that? We went to the same school!

Mike continues: Early in the year I established a simple goal: I was not going down that hole. I spent every lunch period plotting my escape back to the classroom. It involved ducking into certain classrooms, using administrators as shields and every ounce of my energy. As the school year went on the upperclassmen became more and more determined to get me into the hole. My schemes then had to get more elaborate and more desperate. I never went into the hole.

I could have been the only teenage boy who hated lunch. Sadly, when the tennis season started, lunch was the highlight of my day. The tennis team didn't haze me; they tortured me. Playing doubles with a certain one of my teammates was brutal. We were playing our local rival and I was paired up with the teammate who constantly challenged for my spot. He repeatedly would serve the ball into my back. Even though it is a tennis ball, a serve to the back of the head doesn't feel good. This went on with other players I was paired with too.

I had an almost daily toss into the shower (completely clothed of course). On one occasion they wanted to drag me from the tennis court to the shower. It wasn't the shower I resisted; it was the principle of letting them toss me around and demean me. A man has to fight and resist this at all times. So, as they were carrying me through the gate, I grabbed the chain link fencing that surrounded the courts. A teammate was able to get me to let go of the fence by smashing my hand with a tennis racquet and then I was tossed into the shower. It would have been nice if they used hot water instead of cold water. While the hazing of freshmen was essentially seen as an accepted rite of passage in those days, at that point, our team captain deemed the treatment as "too much," brought it to the coach's attention, and the coach decided to put a stop to it all. He called my mom, and told her what had been going on. I had never told my mom because it was too embarrassing. However, to my surprise, it seemed the coaches' call focused on where I was at fault. Apparently, I was constantly bragging about how good I was at tennis and I brought this on myself.

I was a basketball player not a tennis player. My high school valued basketball not tennis. I never once talked about tennis to anyone other than Jay. So, how could I be bragging? The answer is Jay. I believe that to divert attention from himself, he would make me the target by saying things to the upperclassmen on the team. I originally thought I was being tortured because these guys were upset with my sister because she refused to date them. That wasn't the case. It was my friend throwing me under the bus and subsequently into the shower.

Jay responds with passion: Mike and I have had plenty of disagreements -- best friends can't really be best friends unless they get through some shit together in my opinion. However, there are two things that I have been accused of that I will go to my grave with a 100% accurate denial. The first came on a jog that Mike and I went on from McDonald's to his house. This jog probably measured about a half mile (or maybe less). Now it was kind of hot that day, and in the middle of the run, I complained "are we there yet?!!!!" Mike thought this complaint was completely outrageous. In my head, I of course agreed that it was; that was what made the comment funny! I was trying to be funny (my sarcastic Midwest humor was starting to form). Mike continued on about how ridiculous it was that I said that, and as I then tried to explain that I was kidding, Mike would have none of it. To this day, he truly believes that I was being serious. The second came from Mike's insistence that I must have thrown him under the bus to teammates. In his opinion (as I am now understanding more of from above), he couldn't understand any other reason why he would be tortured so much. The truth is that I also didn't understand why he was tortured. And as clearly as I absolutely know that other than being the only other freshman on the varsity team and being somewhat untouchable as the coach's son (thus planting Mike as the sole target of freshmen hazing/torture), I NEVER ONCE told other players about private conversations he and I had about his ability. You see, I agreed with all of what Mike had said regarding his ability. Mike had actually beaten me IN A TOURNAMENT just the fall before this spring season (a loss I did avenge the following January making us 1-1 in tournament play for our careers). I had no reason to "rat him out" because I was always actually rooting for him. But as much as I believe strongly that I wasn't the source of the torture motivation, I also wasn't the solution. I had power then that I didn't use. I wasn't strong enough to use it. I knew what Mike was being faced with, and I didn't do anything to help him.

I do believe now that the first real rift in our friendship may have come from this situation where I was sort of "protected" by the upper classmen because of my coach's son classification, but I honestly felt at the time, that I deserved at least this small benefit because of all the torture I was put through directly from "the coach." However, I often felt badly for the way Mike was treated by the upperclassmen -- especially by the bullies on the team. At that time, the term "bullying" was more of a norm than the trigger word for social injustice that it is today, but nonetheless, I was bothered by what was happening on our team. However, I unfortunately wasn't bothered enough to allow it to alert me in the way it should have. Then, there was the day at Madison High School where I witnessed some gross bullying and for the first time, I became upset. Maybe I noticed more because it was the first time that I ever saw a player go out of his way to torture a teammate, even though the torture gave the opponents a better chance to win (Mike's partner was sacrificing his first serve to try and hit Mike in the back of the head!). Now, I do truly believe that maybe Michael Jordan is the only human in the world more competitive than I am, so it may make a little sense that it would take an act of anti-competitiveness to actually get me to understand that something was just not right, and as sad as it is that it took THAT to get me to notice, at least I was able to grow morally that day as I realized that other people around me were dealing with some bullshit!

Mike retorts: Is that how it works? "I object. No, I object. No No, I passionately object." I guess Jay wins the argument then. Jay likes to dwell on how his dad/coach treated him during his freshman season but I too was suffering. There were many practices where Jay ended up in tears because the coach would scream at him and/or make him run a lot extra. I often wondered which was worse: being tormented by your dad or from your peers. Both stink. My freshman year was my last year playing tennis. Jay thinks I quit because of the juniors on the team, but the truth is I quit because of my feelings towards him and his dad. I decided not to play tennis anymore so I wouldn't resent Jay, which would have surely happened. However, the biggest blow was that phone call that the coach made to my mom. I needed a little protection from the coach, but instead my mom thought I was a jackass.

Jay comes back: I am truly saddened to hear this effect that I had on Mike's tennis career. My dad will be saddened as well. It's a true testament of Mike's character (and I believe the readers will be happy to hear this!) that he is now extremely close to that coach (my dad). Mike is another son to John. I bet many will be surprised to read that. It does stink though because Mike was really good! And I know that he hates tennis (who can blame him now?), so he would say that he couldn't care less that he didn't play after that. He is a self-proclaimed basketball player of course! And I don't know if it matters at all to him, but what Mike doesn't know is that I held a grudge after that day in Madison that lasts even today against that particular partner of his. And, I WAS able to exert a small amount of "revenge" against him in recent years (I am not sure Mike is aware of this or not!). In the summer of 2014 I entered a father/son tournament with my oldest son, Jackson. Jax was 12 at the time, and we competed against sons who were quite a bit older. Now, my tennis level was quite a bit higher than most of the other dads, and this helped me greatly in our semi-final match. I of course wanted to win for Jackson and I, but I also had another goal. I wanted to "punish" Mr. Bully by embarrassing him a bit in front of his son for his actions as a senior in high school. Now, was this the most mature action I have ever allowed myself to execute? Well, definitely not, but I still feel it was a deserved shot to take. So, instead of following the certain "father-son etiquette," I used my ability to simply make Mr. Bully look bad, and while I wouldn't say I enjoyed it, I would say that I felt he deserved to be brought down a few levels that afternoon. Jackson and I dominated, winning 6-1, and we later won the title giving Jackson his first tournament victory in the first tournament he played. The revenge was sweet, but seeing the reaction on Jackson's face when we were about to win, as he just couldn't believe it, was truly priceless.

QUITTING IS HABITUAL

Mike returns: I think Jay needs to fence this discussion and I need to clean it. But first some clarification is needed. I don't know what "self-proclaimed basketball player" means. I was on the basketball team; I did have a uniform; I was in the team picture, and from time to time I got in the scoring column. If it walks like a duck and quacks like a duck …

> **Jay responds:** I believe that athletes that play multiple sports often claim that they are a certain type of player. I once had a great athlete/player at Bowling Green, Nick Moxley. Nick was the only guy on the team who could challenge me on the basketball court. During an amazing spring trip to LA/Vegas, we were playing the 30th ranked South Carolina Gamecocks (how can they be called the Cocks but the Indians can't be the Indians anymore?). Anyway, after winning his match at #4 singles over a player who was highly favored by the Vegas bookies, Nick said during the handshake, "Congrats, you just lost to a basketball player." He was a "self-proclaimed basketball player." I believe I am too! That's what I mean Michael…

Mike continues: Next, to the bottom of the mystery of how the tennis team knew of the conversations between Jay and myself. I can think of three potential possibilities. First, Jay told them.

> **Jay:** Nope!

Mike: Second, Jay told his dad about them. Third, hidden microphones. If Jay denies the first and the third is absurd, then the second is the best option. I am sure Coach John Harris noticed how the team was treating me. Coach Harris probably asked Jay for some insight on the situation. So, Jay told his dad about our conversation and Coach Harris made the assumption that the team knew about these conversations.

Jay: Ok, that's a possibility. In 1986, hidden recording devices were often placed in high school classrooms in an effort to... ok just kidding. Yes, there is a possibility that I told my dad about certain convos Mike and I had. And I suppose my dad could have conveyed some of that to the players. I could imagine him using it as a motivation for them. He could have said: "Andy, you gonna let this little kid take your spot? He thinks it should be his, you know..."

Mike continues: The amazing thing is that none of the above matters. My life turned out just fine. I don't care about that tennis team. I don't hold a grudge toward any of the players. I wish them all well. I refuse to live my life dwelling on what could have been. One of those teammates had several kids that I have taught and they were some of my favorite students.

Jay comes back: As with many conversations with Mike and I, they do go off on certain tangents and we actually sometimes forget what the hell we were actually talking about! I guess the nice thing about writing this book together though is that we can just look back at "what the hell we were talking about?" Ha So, this all started with a conversation about quitting. I do agree with Michael Jordan that "quitting will become a habit if you do it once," so I have always believed that a person should never quit. Now, I will clarify that quitting a sport at the end of a season after being tortured does NOT classify as quitting, nor does quitting a marriage where one has to endure true emotional torture daily, especially after giving the marriage every chance possible.

The type of quitting that bothers me, is the quitting when things get a little tough, or even pretty tough. With tennis players I see this sort of "softness" all the time. A player loses a first set and goes down a break in the second, and all of a sudden, he/she has a life-threatening injury (eye roll emoji would be great to insert here!). Or my favorite (meaning least favorite) occurs when a player is down a set and like 5-1 and then "retires" (another word in tennis for QUITS). That player couldn't just stand there for one more minute and allow his/her opponent to win the last four points? I mean come on! I have never retired from one match in my life. I have never quit in the middle of any basketball game (and during one game I broke my arm but didn't even come out - I could still walk I would tell Mr. Favre!). I have only missed one day of work in the past 35 years and that was because I had a triple hernia operation that day -- I DID go to work the day after because again, I was able to walk (kind of!). And yes, I AM knocking on wood right now as I state all of these things! Not quitting is an incredible habit. It takes toughness for sure, but mostly it takes patience. Patience has become possibly my biggest strength as a person, and also at times my biggest weakness. But patience in sport is almost as key as confidence. There are so many clichés of course. "It's not how you fall, but how you get up" is one of my favorites. Quitting in my opinion is the ultimate loss, and not coincidentally, making an opponent quit is what I call the ultimate win. It is the breaking of someone's character. To me that means more than just being better at a sport than someone, and I believe the ultimate competitors, while they want to work to be great at their craft, truly desire to break the spirit of those they compete against by imposing their will, and by being patient enough to hang in there until doing so. A quote that is attributed to Michael Jordan but I believe was said first by Jimmy Connors is: "I have never lost; I have only run out of time to win." That is true toughness, true patience, and that mentality would only come from an athlete who would NEVER QUIT. As the infamous Jimmy Valvano said: "Don't give up...don't ever give up."

Mike adds in: Jay and I watched Young Guns II when I was too impressionable. There is a scene in the movie that encapsulates my position on playing games. Billy the Kid is trying to give an inspirational talk to his gang when he tells a story about three

Chinamen playing Fan-Tan. As the story goes: the world was about to end when one man said he was going on a mission to pray. Another man says that he was going to a brothel. The third man says that he was going to finish the game. It is the third man that I believe got it right. It is a real challenge for me not to complete anything. I play the game until it is over. I stay in church until the choir is done singing. I stay in the movie theater until the final credits roll.

Too many times players want to quit when they are losing or when things are getting tough. NBA legend Reggie Miller once scored eight points in the final nine seconds to win a playoff game. Utah Jazz player Paul Millsap scored 11 points in 28 seconds to win a game. The Lakers scored the final 14 points in the remaining 50 seconds to beat the Kings in 2007. It is really easy to give up during the course of a game, but it is vital to finish the game. If a player quits just once, the second time will be easier, and the third time even easier. Great comebacks like Reggie Miller produced are rare, but the importance of the constant battle is essential to success.

I was coaching girls' basketball and there was a girl who was maybe 5'2" who had a father who thought she was the next Sue Bird. The player wasn't fast, she was a poor shooter, and she refused to be a ball handler. Her father absolutely insisted she was not only a varsity player but the best player on the team. He was in the Athletic Office weekly with complaints about me and how I was holding his daughter back. I made a huge mistake by not being completely honest with him. He once told me that I "crushed her." The truth is that I didn't want to crush him. He loved his daughter and wanted to protect her. She had given up on the team long before. She once intentionally shot the ball over the entire basket. She ran through drills at half speed. She refused to participate in a fun end-of-practice drill. The bottom line was that she didn't receive immediate success, she didn't get what she wanted, and she wasn't willing to work for it. I have no idea what she was telling her father but it wasn't the truth. She wanted instant gratification and when it didn't come she gave up.

Quitting isn't always just turning in the uniform and walking away from a team. It usually starts long before the uniform is laid on the coach's desk. The quitting starts when a player shows up to practice late. Quitting starts when a player is running a line drill and doesn't go all the way to the line. Quitting starts when the coach asks you to make 50 putts and the player makes 30 putts. Quitting starts when the backup quarterback complains to a teammate that he should be the starting quarterback. Coaches see all of these actions and hear all of the comments. What a player is doing is setting the stage to quit. The foundation is based on excuses for failure. The moment when a player doesn't commit fully to a perfect practice or to support the team, he or she has quit.

Coaches see these actions and I hope they have conversations with the player to stop the trend toward quitting. Typical coaches are going to tell the player how much they mean to the team; "the team needs you"; "with a little more effort and work and you will get more playing time"; "stay positive and your time will come." These are the standard coaching clichés, and they hold water. They may be applicable to the player. They should make the player feel good, but they won't always stop the trend toward quitting. It takes a certain team culture to do that.

The best way to avoid quitting is to have the proper and realistic mindset. However, a good support structure is important. One of the many discussions that Jay and I have had is the topic of Tom Brady. Remember, Jay coached at Brown University, just a stone's throw from Foxboro. I am the son and step-son of an Ohio State alum and I am an Ohio State alum. Jay hates Tom Brady and I think he is the GOAT. It isn't easy to admit a player from that team up north is the GOAT, but I refuse to ignore facts. And fact number one is that Tom Brady has a fist full of Super Bowl rings and two to spare. Jay and I have debated too much on the greatness of Brady but rather a big "what if?" With the 183rd pick in the 2000 NFL Draft the Cleveland Browns selected Spergon Wynn from Southwest Texas State. With the 199th pick the New England Patriots selected Tom Brady.

Would Tom Brady still be the GOAT if the Browns would have drafted him? Remember the Browns didn't exist for three years and the first season they returned to the field was 1999. The Browns were 2-14 in their restart. They drafted Tim Couch from the University of Kentucky to be their savior. The Browns did not pay much attention to their offensive line and Couch was annihilated. Could Brady have avoided that fate and become the GOAT? I always argue that Brady would have just been one of the 30 (and counting) starting quarterbacks that the Browns have had since 1999.

The New England Patriots were an organization with stability in ownership, stability in the front office, and stability in the coaching staff. The Cleveland Browns were the exact opposite of that organization. The Patriots had an experienced veteran quarterback willing to help Brady. Their coaching staff had clear expectations and team structure to help the individual players. The Patriots had an environment conducive to winning. I am a believer that winning fixes a lot of problems. When a team is successful the individual player will practice better, prepare better, perform better and be better. His mindset will be far from quitting.

Quitters are typically "tourists." There is a certain type of person that I describe as a tourist. A tourist is a person that drifts in and out of situations and the lives of other people. They never stick around to get committed to anything or anyone. I had a player on my team this season that as a sophomore decided she wanted to play golf. Great, I was glad to add her to the team. I was glad to add her because she is a personality. She smiles a lot, helps other players with their self-esteem, and is a good teammate. She was not a good golfer. After the season, she said she wasn't going to play next year. Instead, she was going to play tennis. Of course I asked why the change. She told me she wants to play a different sport each season.

I have noticed that many very nice student-athletes are tourists. They play a sport but they don't commit to it. I don't care what a person does, but do it well. Don't be a tourist in a sport; go all-in. A golfer should watch golf, they should understand the history;

they should know the past greats and who is going to be the next Nicklaus (Woods for the younger crowd); they need to go all in. Tourists are nice, but their methodology doesn't put them on a path towards success.

Jay tells yet another story: I love the descriptions of quitting here. Mike is right. It's not just stopping what you are doing. It starts with giving a bad effort. One of my favorite students will likely always be at least partially known by me as the 9 push-up guy. Aiden is a super talented tennis player, but he often gets in his own way to essentially halt his success. We are working hard on it though and he is making some great progress. A few years ago, we were at a lesson and I asked him if he could do ten push-ups. He replied, "I don't know." Aiden is very honest! I then said, "Okay, let's see!" So, Aiden assumed the position and started pounding out military-form push-ups like it was his job. I counted out loud: "six, seven, eight, nine" and it happened. He went down for that tenth push-up and started to push up, but then stopped and his chest collapsed to the ground. I was like, "Wait, what happened?!" And Aiden replied, "It was too hard." I couldn't understand! He did nine perfect push-ups and then just stopped. So, we talked about what had happened for about five minutes. I did what I thought was some great motivating and then asked if he wanted to try again. He said yes! So there we go. I was counting again: "seven, eight, nine" and it happened again!! What the heck. He was a push-up pro for nine straight push-ups and then just stopped. The truth is, it got a little tough, and he quit. Good news is that he became aware of this flaw, corrected it, and is now a very successful college tennis player.

A new favorite player of mine, Mia, currently nine-years-old as I type some final edits for this book, seems to have a different approach already. In a recent lesson, I hit a very wide ball to her forehand side and then came into the net. Mia hit a solid passing shot but I was able to reach for a volley and produce a very sharp angle, short to the opposite side of the court. As Mia ran for the ball which continued to angle off the court and towards the side wall, I said to myself: "ok Mia, you can't get that one. Let it go." However, Mia definitely didn't have that same inner dialogue. She got to the ball and hit it back into the court and then literally went head first into the wall! She for sure didn't think of quitting there, and I am excited for her potential, as I am predicting that this trait will help her produce much success! Hopefully no more crashes into walls though Mia!!

Why did Mike and I not have that quitting gene in us? I don't know about Mike, but I remember the exact day it was eliminated from my being. My grandfather had made a ping pong table and we had it in our garage. I was about nine years old on this fateful day. My dad challenged me to a game. Now he was much much better than me, so he told me that he would give me an 18-0 lead, and we would play to 21. He also said that we would play for $1. This was my first official bet, and I'm just realizing as I type why I now hate gambling so much! We played the first game and I somehow won! I WAS given an 18-0 lead of course, but still. My dad then said, "Okay, double or nothing." Being nine in 1980, a dollar was good, but two bucks would be pretty solid! So I agreed and won again! He then said, "Double or nothing?" I agreed and won! Four bucks! It happened again. Eight dollars! And again, 16 bucks!! This may have equaled my career income at that time. My dad said double or nothing again but this time it wasn't as much of a question I noticed. I agreed and won. And then won again. $64. He said double or nothing and I said, "Nope, I'm good." He then pleaded. I said no. The pleading became a bit more demanding. So I agreed. I won that game, $128. These were like career earnings figures to me at that time! I won, celebrated and began a march inside. He said "Get back here, double or nothing." A Midwest boy in this era does NOT disobey his dad. So I played, with tears in my eyes, and won again. I was up to $256, but I knew the end of this story already. He said, "double or nothing." I said nothing and got into ready position and then proceeded to lose 21-18. I put the paddle down, went inside and cried myself to sleep. In reality, I hadn't really lost anything, but good luck convincing me of that then. I learned two valuable lessons that day. First, losing hurts a lot, and second, no matter how afraid I am to lose, I'm NEVER allowed to quit. Thanks dad for that one!

MAKE YOUR LAST SHOT ALWAYS

It is not the mountain we conquer but ourselves.

—Edmund Hillary

Growing up in Ohio where high school sports create a certain sort of intense passion allowed me the opportunity to experience so many incredible moments, and many of them, if not most of them, were inside the confines of some high school gym in some remote little town in Ohio. My dad, being the intense high school basketball coach that he was, allowed me to tag along to many practices and hundreds of games. I have of course gotten to see his coaching style, and witnessed how the players reacted to his style versus many other coaching styles. I think what all of those experiences instilled in me was an intense passion for Sport. When you have this sort of passion, you learn to work to do everything you can to put yourself and your team in a position to win! And when I say everything you can do, I really mean that, and one aspect of that work, is a bit of superstition. One day I was in the gym at Cardington High School, and I was shooting around after practice; the team had gone into the locker room to shower, mess around or do whatever they were doing in there, and my dad went into his office to talk to the coaches maybe about how practice went I guess, and so I was in the gym by myself just shooting around. I was about ten years old at the time. Not too long after, the starting point guard came out into the gym. He walked over to watch me shoot and gave me a couple shooting tips. I actually wish I remembered those shooting tips today! It was really nice of him to do that of course. But what stood out the most and actually still lives with me today was one particular tip. I was essentially done shooting as I knew my dad would be coming into the gym soon and be ready to drive home. And so I shot one last shot, missed it, and then went to put the ball away. All of a sudden the point guard was like, "Whoa whoa whoa, what are you doing?" and I was like," I'm putting the ball away." He then exclaimed "ABSOLUTELY NOT! You do not miss your last shot!" I stopped in my tracks, and then he explained to me why you don't miss your last shot. He said, "You never want to leave the gym on a bad note. Whatever happens in the gym whether it's a good day, a bad day, or an OK day, you always need to end on a good note." I also now often preach using the cliché, "It's not about how you start, it's how you finish." Maybe that's what the point guard was telling me that time. Maybe that was my first lesson in finishing strong. But it's a lesson that still holds true today. From that moment as a 10-year-old, to now, never have I left the gym without making my last shot. And I've been in a lot of gyms! I've even at times made that last shot with a crumpled up paper cup because there wasn't a basketball around to shoot. But nonetheless I made that last shot. I finished strong. Always. That habit has even carried over to the tennis court. If I lost the match and missed the last shot of the match which of course happens often, at some point before I leave the court, I simply hit a ball onto the other side inside the boundaries of the court, making that last shot. I'm now on a tennis court almost every day of my life. I always make the last shot.

Mike responds: I agree with Jay but I would take it a step further and say make your first shot too. When I was playing basketball or coaching basketball I always made my first shot. I would walk out of the locker room, grab a ball off the rack and walk to the block by the basket, take a deep breath and make the little bank shot. I always wanted to put a positive thought in my head. As a person who works in a proshop at a public golf course I am witness to many poor decisions. Unfortunately, people try to sneak on the course, steal range balls, and hawk at the range. A hawk is someone who doesn't buy a bag of range balls; instead, they wait until someone leaves range balls behind and hits them. The one type of person I never get frustrated with is the person that hits their bag of balls at the range and then walks into the range to grab an extra ball or two. When a person has 75 balls in a range bag, what happens when the 75th ball is a shank? Of course, the player has to grab another ball and swing again. This shows me the player is there to get better.

Too many players arrive at the practice range to hit golf balls. This is not the right approach if a player wants to improve and wants to win. A player has to go to the practice range to get better, not just hit balls.

> **Jay asks:** So Mike, can you walk our many fans that are now avid golfers through how to use the making your first and last shot methods on the range?

Mike responds: I will start with how to make their first shot. When I am going to work at the range I choose my spot carefully. The range I use the most has me hitting to the north. This means the wind is typically pushing from the left to the right. I either stay to the far left edge of the range and aim back right. Or, I go to the far right side and aim to the back left. The only time I set up right in the middle is when the wind is due north or south. By setting up to reduce the effect of the wind on the golf ball I will get a better understanding of what my swing is doing. Before hitting my first shot I always do some basic stretch work. At my age this has become a necessity. I normally take my 3 iron and my 4 iron out of the bag and use them to aid my stretching routine. I only spend five to seven minutes doing this. Once my body feels good, I take those two clubs and hold them together and do some swinging.

The purpose of the pre-practice routine is to get my mind ready to perform well. If I just take the bag of balls and dump the balls out onto the range and start swinging away, I am not prepared for success. Most players I see at the range aren't there to get better. They are just happy hackers who should skip the range, grab a cooler of beer, and proceed to the back tees because they are just "that good." These players will also have their music turned up so loud that it can be heard two holes away. If a player goes to the range wanting to play well, then they should be there to get better at the game. This means no music and no airpods. Understanding the golf swing includes both sound and feel. When I hit the ball in the center of the club face, it sounds different than if I am slightly left or right of center. Music doesn't belong on the practice range.

Now that I am mentally and physically ready to practice, I grab my pitching wedge and take some half swings with it. I then pick a target about 70 yards out on the range. My stock wedge shot is 140 yards. So I pick an easy shot to execute, much like a layup in basketball. I hit two or three of these half to three quarter shots and then start my full swing. I will mix things up to keep the wear and tear on my irons the same. I am a school teacher and I can't afford to buy new Titleist irons every year. One day I will use the even numbered clubs and the next range session I use the odd numbered clubs. I start with the short irons and work my way down to the driver. Every shot I hit, I have a specific target. I never just hit a ball without some degree of thought. At some point during the middle of the range session, I will hit some punch shots and I will hit some fades and draws. When I really want to get serious about a practice session, I will visualize specific golf holes, and I will play those holes. If I know I am playing Shelby Country Club, then I think about some difficult tee shots where I will have to shape the shot. I then hit some of those tee shots.

Now it's time to make my "last shot." When I get down to three to five balls remaining, I pick a shot with a short iron. This is a very specific shot. I use my range finder and get the precise number where I want the ball to land. I then pick the right club for that distance and I start my pre shot routine. I treat the last shot as if I were competing at the Masters. I then hit until I make the shot and when I make the shot, it is my last, and I am done.

Jay takes a last shot: I love it Mike as I am going to implement all of that into my practice rituals on the range! I also wanted to finish this up with one more story about first and last shots. When I was in high school and college, I was a pretty good competitor. However, I was far from perfect, and in looking back, especially knowing what I know now, it is actually funny to think about a few of the ridiculous things I used to do. Possibly the dumbest was in the way I used to warm up my serve for matches, and how that warm-up affected my match mentality.

A tennis match usually starts with a cooperative warm-up between the two opponents (or four in doubles). This may seem strange to many in other sports, and this opponent warm-up has recently been done away with in college tennis, but nonetheless, this is how most matches do start, even on the pro tour. After hitting groundstrokes and volleys for a few minutes, players will warm up their own serves. What I used to do during this portion of the warm-up is something that anyone would be forced to question my intelligence. I would step up to hit my first warm-up serve, and I would tell myself that if I hit a good serve with this first one, then great, I will probably serve and play well in the match. However, if I hit a bad serve, then I immediately assumed that I would serve terribly and also play pretty poorly. This teetering was essentially all based on ONE serve, a serve that I wasn't even loose enough to hit well! After reading this chapter, it is easy to see that this was NOT the right way to handle this. What I needed to do was make the first one, probably with a small amount of pace, then build up to where I felt good physically, then hit a few of those with accuracy, and then make sure to make my last one. Doing all of this would help me to start the match with the proper mindset.

THE NATURE OF THE SPORT COMEBACK

It ain't over 'til it's over

—Unknown

There are many great comebacks to evaluate. The Cleveland Indians came back after trailing by 12 going into the 7th inning. The Vikings overcame a 33-point deficit. Paul Lawrie overcame a 10 stroke deficit to win the British Open. The Colts overcame a 21-point deficit in the final four minutes to beat the Buccaneers. No matter what comeback I would choose to evaluate, I would end up with the same questions. Did one team choke or did a team simply outperform because they were more focused?

I often wonder why broadcasters talk about the first four minutes of each half in football being the most important. I understand that teams want to get off to good starts, but a college football game is 48 minutes long. The amount of time that broadcasters are discussing is just 16% of the game. On October 14, 1984, Ohio State was playing Illinois and the Buckeyes got off to a horrendous start. They fell behind 17-0 in the first quarter, and 24-0 early in the second quarter. Ohio State looked terrible. Running back Keith Byars flat out fumbled without anyone touching him. Then Keith Byars scored a touchdown with five minutes to go in the half. Byars announced to the cameraman that they were "coming back." The Buckeyes recovered an onside kick and then scored again on a great catch by Cris Carter to be down just 10 points. The Buckeyes got the ball back with about two minutes to go in the half, and Byars got his second touchdown and they went to halftime down just three points. The Buckeyes kicked off to start the second half and the Illini fumbled it to OSU.

The Buckeyes matriculated the ball down the field and Byars leapt over the line getting his third touchdown. The Buckeyes led 28-24. Illinois countered with a field goal and then one of the greatest plays ever happened. On Ohio State's next possession Keith Byars ran out of his shoe for a 70-yard touchdown. The Buckeyes never looked back and won 45-38. Byars ran for 274 yards and 5 touchdowns. On a side note, Byars not winning the Heisman that year was criminal.

Momentum, momentum, and momentum. Did OSU get it after the first touchdown, the onside kick recovery, or with Byars prophecy of the comeback? What mentally changed for the Illini? What mentally changed for the Buckeyes? Is it easier to play from behind or ahead?

Jay responds: A tennis coach once told me that I needed to select different shots when I was ahead as compared to when I was behind because my hands would work much better when I was behind. What the heck was he talking about?!

The answer actually comes from the world of physiology. When a person is under stress, blood flow is often reduced because of the restriction of blood vessels caused by the body's reaction to the perceived stress. Coming back to the comment about the hands, it does make sense that a reduced blood flow would cause less feel with the hands and essentially make an athlete's hands not work as well. Anyone who watches college basketball's March Madness has witnessed this in full effect, especially when a higher seed is on the ropes and the underdog is in striking distance. In 2023, for the second time in the history of the NCAA basketball tournament, a #1 seed lost to a #16 seed. The Purdue Boilermakers, led by their 7'4" center, Zach Edey, came into their first round game against Fairleigh Dickinson as a 23-point favorite. The FDU Knights were literally the smallest team of all Division I teams in the country, but it didn't matter. Their blood was flowing like an adrenaline filled tiger chasing prey, while the vessels inside of the Boilermakers became continuously tighter as the game progressed. Purdue was not ready for a battle, and when they found themselves in one late in the game instead of the blowout victory they expected, their physical states actually made them the underdogs. While basketball can of course be a game of physicality and strength, it is still a game of technique and shot mechanics. Understanding all of this, it is not surprising to find out that Purdue shot just 36% from the field in this particular game and lost what many feel is the biggest upset in college basketball history. Their hands simply did not work!

I want to circle back to how this "hands business" works in a comeback. When a team is ahead and in the *building a lead mode*, they are often just playing the game. The blood is flowing beautifully; their muscles are loose; they are playing for "The Love of the Game." However, if they take their attention away from the process that has helped them build the lead, and especially if the majority of their focus turns to the actual score, or the clock, then their performance level will almost certainly drop. This is magnified when the opposing team gets in *back against the wall mode*. That team's blood may not have been in a nice flow early in the game, but all of a sudden, they get a spark. Maybe one of the guys hit a three and then another guy grabbed a steal and a bucket. After the spark, the team behind may notice that their opponent is getting "tight", and then all of a sudden, it is like sharks in the water smelling blood. An underdog, like the FDU Knights, are swarming all over the court, and the favorite, like Purdue, is simply trying to survive.

Basketball is a sport that has a built in momentum buster, the timeout. When a team goes on a run, the coach being victimized by the run often will call a timeout. It's a time to settle the team down, maybe reinvigorate the blood flow, and get them focused on the process. Mike, as a former high school basketball coach, has used this method countless times. However, not all sports have this option. Now, in football, there is an option to call a timeout, and while it is sometimes used to settle a team down, it is more often saved and/or used to reserve time at the end of a half or game.

In other sports, like tennis, there isn't a timeout option, BUT many players still find a way to get one at times. Recently, there has been a lot of controversy in professional tennis surrounding the topic of the bathroom break. Growing up playing junior tennis, I was well aware of the "art" of taking a bathroom break. Knowing that there are no timeouts allowed in tennis, a "smart" player may realize that there are also no rules against taking a bathroom break, and thus, when feeling the need to stop a run by an opponent, the player will simply go to the bathroom. Now, while a basketball timeout is usually no more than a couple of minutes, a tennis bathroom break could be five to ten minutes, or even more! There is a famous scene in the movie *King Richard*, the Williams sisters' story, where in her first professional tournament, Venus was beating the #2 player in the world, Arantxa Sanchez-Vicario, when she took an egregious bathroom break, leaving the court for 18 minutes, essentially freezing the 14 year-old Venus, and when play resumed, the veteran dominated play.

In 2010, I moved to New York to work for Sportime, the home of the John McEnroe Tennis Academy. My first boss there was a former professional player, Eric Fromm. In a two-year span, Eric taught me a ton about business, as he was extremely intelligent, and held an MBA from Columbia University to prove it. At the end of my first year, a highly successful one for the clubs that I managed, it was time for me to sit down with Eric and discuss a potential bonus and raise for the following fiscal year. At the beginning of the meeting, I had told Eric that I only had 45 minutes because a new family was coming in to meet with me to check out the club. Yes, I set that up on purpose so as not to give Eric too much time to drag this meeting out. So, after about 35 minutes of going back and forth discussing and arguing about "my worth," I reminded Eric that we only had ten minutes left. I then picked up the pace of the discussion, firing a slew of prepared points like they were huge forehands penetrating the court. All of a sudden Eric stopped and said: "I have to go to the bathroom." I of course was thinking: oldest trick in the book! I was ready. When Eric came back to the table I said to him: Eric, you know when a tennis player is up 4-1 in the third, and then the other guy takes a bathroom break? Eric replied: "of course." I continued: One of two things happen, right? Either the guy steals the momentum and comes back to win, or the player in the lead holds his nerve and pulls out the set. I'm the type of guy who laughs at the guy taking the bathroom break and when he comes back, punishes him for making him wait by winning the last two games quickly to win that third set 6-1. I then slid a notecard across the table to Eric and said: This is what I want. Eric looked at my proposed new salary and bonus with a look that was mixed with astonishment and respect, and simply said: "I'm going to have to talk to Claude (Sportime's owner) about this." I said: I'm sure you do. Days later, I was granted my requests. The comeback was thwarted!

Mike finishes up: When people talk about sports comebacks they focus on the team behind in the game. People want to focus on what the trailing team did to complete the comeback. As Jay mentioned earlier, Purdue was in a complete meltdown because of the pressure. The pressure came in not just being the overwhelming favorite but the tempo in which FDU was playing. They didn't allow Purdue to have a *bathroom break*. Teams and players that are leading in contests should never allow a bathroom break.

I know people are more likely to remember the comeback story because they are rare. More often than not the comeback is thwarted. What allows a team in the lead to stay in the lead? The answer is pressure. Teams need to continue to work the game plan from the start to the finish. Players in individual sports need to do the same. In the 2023 Masters Tournament, Brooks Koepka held the 54-hole lead. In the final round he played very conservatively, and finished tied for second place with Phil Mickelson. Nearly two months later, Koepka was competing at the PGA. In an interview, Koepka admitted that he didn't like his final round approach at the Masters. For the final round at the PGA, Koepka stayed with his assertive game plan and was able to win the tournament. In Koepka's words he was playing not to lose the Masters Tournament whereas at the PGA, Koepka played to win. I prefer to play to win instead of not to lose. When I have a lead I try to keep the pressure on my opponent until the very end of the game. If I lose I want to know that I did all I could to win.

One of the things that I look at to assess my golfer's mental state is their right thumb. I teach that the right thumb should lightly lay over top of the club shaft (this is assuming the player is right handed). Players really just need three fingers on the club and the thumb provides a little support but is really along for the ride. A drill I teach is to have the players take swings with the thumb raised. This helps the player get the club along the fingers and off the palm. It also forces a better tempo. When I look at the player's right thumb and I see that it is pressing on the shaft I know they are carrying some tension or stress. Just as in tennis, a golfer needs to have soft hands. A player must allow the blood to flow. I have been in some pressure golf situations and the trick I use to keep the blood vessels open is to regrip a few times before each shot.

I am not a player that takes many practice swings and I have very little waggle. The only time I take practice swings is on shots 100 yards or less. These are the feel shots and I try to create the right feel before I make my shot. All other swings are stock swings and I just trust my preparation. Now in pressure matches (meaning there is money at stake), I will get set over the ball and then release my hands and then regrip with a lighter grip and then I will do it again. One of my pre-shot checkpoints are my forearms. If I look down and see my veins popping out I know I am too tight. When I re-grip the club it releases the tension I am carrying in my hands and forearms.

POETRY OF SELF-TALK

You become what you think about.

—Napoleon Hill

The way you think influences the way you feel and the way you feel determines how you act.

—Craig Sager

It is important for all of us to push ourselves to be successful, but it is equally, if not more important, for us to be self-advocates. Meaning, it is important for us to be encouraging and very supportive of ourselves.

—Jay Harris

In the 1990s, the science of sport psychology began to take center stage. Dr. Jim Loehr was known as one of the world's most gifted consultants as he often wrote about mental toughness and originally focused a lot of his efforts on tennis players as he was famous for the "16-second cure," which was a method for tennis players to follow in between points in order to enhance their performance during point play. Then, in 1994, Loehr helped bring sport psych more into the mainstream sports world as he was the lead consultant who helped speed skater Dan Jansen (the GOAT of skating at the time) overcome a 10-year Olympic jinx and capture what may have been the most emotional gold medal win since the 1980 *Miracle on Ice*.

During that time period, I was going through my junior and then college tennis career myself, and I would often hear from coaches about the importance of staying positive. As much as that of course makes sense, I often hated it. If I just missed an easy shot, it didn't make all that much sense to me to just be like "oh Jay, it's okay that you just shanked that ball. Don't worry. You'll get the next one." However, I did listen to many of the coaches and I also read the recommendations from some of the leading sports psychologists like Dr. Loehr, and thus, I did implement some positive self-talk into my own rituals. This would come to help me greatly in the spring of 1989.

I was a senior in high school navigating through a tennis season where I was able to take down multiple nationally ranked players, and I had one big goal in mind which was to qualify for the State Tournament. To do so, I would need to finish in the top three in the District Tourney, which was held in Bowling Green, Ohio (coincidentally on courts I would later serve as the head men's tennis coach!). I came into the tournament on a bit of a roll and won my first two matches easily, setting up a semifinal showdown with German exchange student, Lars Bleeker. Lars had also been on a roll and I would say was the favorite in our match-up. However, I played almost perfect tennis and went up 6-4, 5-2, 40-love, a single point away from achieving my biggest life goal up to that date. That's when I was hit with an avalanche of emotions that I was simply not equipped to handle. I began to tell my teammates that were standing just off the court cheering me on how nervous I was. I felt my entire body shaking. I missed a return making the score 15-40. Lars shanked an overhead winner into the corner to make it 30-40. Then, after I hit another very tentative return, Lars came in on a rather vanilla approach to my backhand, and I somehow steered the easy pass just an inch wide to even the score of that game at deuce. After missing two more shots to make the score 5-3, the snowball of nerves just continued to get bigger and bigger and before I knew it, I had lost that set

7-6, and then the third 6-4, and my chances to qualify for State were going to have to be transferred into a third/fourth playoff match against a junior rival of mine, Brad Emmons.

I had beaten Brad twice in the two weeks leading up to this district tournament, and one of those wins was actually a 6-0, 6-0 beatdown. I still don't know how I beat him 0 & 0 because Brad was actually very good. He later played #1 for the University of Toledo, so he was no slouch. I knew this going into the huge playoff and qualifying match, but I also knew that I was supposed to win. Walking on to the court just 45 minutes after the gut-wrenching loss to Lars, I honestly did not feel good. I was sick to my stomach. All I could think about was the huge choke that I just produced. Not surprisingly, I did not get off to a good start. I went down 3-0 and Brad was looking more and more confident in his chances. My dad, Coach Harris, who would usually come and yell at me at this point in any match, was so taken aback with what had transpired the match before, that not even HE knew what to say! It was the first time I ever saw my dad literally speechless. I was a bit confused out there by myself on the court, but then, almost as an epiphany, I had a brilliant idea. I decided that no matter what happened, I would say, OUT LOUD, something positive. If I missed a shot, I would say "nice try." If I hit a good shot, I would say "great ball" This isn't something I had ever really tried to consistently do on the court, but I was desperate. As the first set wore on, I started to feel a bit less queasy in my stomach. It did help that Brad got a little tight himself with the lead that he had managed to build, but my positive self-talk mechanism was working wonders on my own head! I started to feel more and more confident, and once I got back to even at 3-3 in the first set, I actually knew I would win. I did win that match 6-3, 6-3 which gave me a berth into the State Tennis Tournament, an important life goal.

Mike responds: Stay positive! Wow, what a great idea, Jay. I think every athlete knows this piece of advice. For a coach it is the most difficult thing to teach a player. During most athletic competitions there are far more negative actions than positive. In football, when a quarterback attempts a pass only one good thing can happen (outside of penalties); everything else is bad. In NCAA men's basketball only 10teams are currently shooting over 50% from the field (December 22, 2021). In baseball, a batter is considered good if he gets a hit three out of 10 at bats. A PGA tour player hits a green in regulation from under 200 yards just 50% of the time. I can address every sport with similar stat lines. The bottom line in athletics is that more can go wrong than right. So staying positive is a challenge.

> **Jay comes back:** My favorite movie is a baseball movie starring Kevin Costner and it isn't *Bull Durham* or *Field of Dreams*. It is actually *For Love of the Game*. In my opinion, it is one of the most underrated movies ever as one would be hard pressed to find someone who even lists this movie in their top 50. Mike, we should possibly share our top 25 movies in our next book! Okay, back to the movie – Costner plays an aging major league pitcher and it chronicles his baseball career as he recants it while he is pitching in a late season game against the Yankees. This game takes place in the "house that Ruth built," Yankee Stadium, and the fans were of course loud and obnoxious, as many Yankees' fans are! I am a Red Sox fan by the way so I can say that!
>
> One cool aspect about the movie for me is that there is a great deal of sports psychology written into it. In one particular scene, Costner's character, Billy Chapel, is standing on the mound, getting ready to throw a pitch, and he notices the crowd screaming and yelling. He then focuses on the catcher and says the words "clear the mechanism." In an instant, all of the crowd noise and even images fade away and he can only see the line to the catcher. He buries a pitch into the catcher's mitt for strike one, and then the crowd noise comes back. Chapel's "clear the mechanism

technique" is a great example of self-talk. He had developed the ability to block out any distractions by attaching this short phrase to a deep state of concentration.

Mike comes back in: I'm not sure Costner can make a bad movie. Even *Water World* had some merit. I do agree with Jay that For *Love of the Game* is the better baseball movie for mostly the same reasons. I also appreciate how Chapel signed the baseball and sent it to the GM announcing his retirement from the game. The poetry of Chapel's self-talk is in the simplicity. Unfortunately, too many athletes make self-talk very complicated and more often, negative self-talk.

When an athlete's self-confidence is low, almost every little thing triggers negative self-talk. If a tennis player is on clay courts and is trailing in the match, a bad bounce can easily trigger negative self-talk. I remember a tennis match nearly 40 years ago during the Miss Ohio tournament. Jay had a terrible draw and had to play me in the semis. It has been a long time since I have played in a tennis tournament and things may have changed, but back then, each player brought a new can of balls. One can would be used during the match and the winner would take the unopened can to the next match. Jay was a little over confident and didn't bring a can of tennis balls. The match started very poorly for Jay. I got up early and the self-talk was off and running. Typically, self-talk is internal, but that isn't Jay's style. Every time he hit a ball long he thought I was hooking him (a tennis word for cheating). Then in the second set (after I won the first), I hit a serve that hit the tape and took a wicked bad bounce. Jay threw a tantrum that made him begin to unravel. Jay did not have a "clear mechanism" tool at his disposal, and my skills were just too much to overcome! Bad bounces are a part of almost every sport. They are something that cannot be controlled and a strong competitor will not allow these instances to affect self-talk in a negative way. So, what is the secret to good self-talk?

Jay responds: I knew that loss would come back to haunt me! Yes, I lost to Mike 7-5, 7-5, and yes, it was a "soft" competitive performance by me. Thank goodness that Mike played one last tournament about a year later, just before his tennis retirement. In that tournament, I got another "bad draw," and was forced to play Mike again. I won that one 6-1, 6-0. My self-talk was definitely better in that one!

In my opinion, the real secret to self-talk starts with competitiveness. I realize this may be a strange answer to some, but hear me out. The most competitive athletes will want to do anything they can to put themselves in a position to win. When I say anything, I really mean *anything*! These super competitive people will have an understanding that constructive self-talk leads to improved performance, and thus, they will work hard to produce self-talk that is exactly that ... constructive! I'll use a contrarian example.

Nick Kyrgios is one of the most talented tennis players I have ever seen. His results have been extremely up and down, but he is one of the only pros on tour who has beaten all of the "big three" (arguably the best three players of all time) – Federer, Djokovic and Nadal. Until this past summer, Kyrgios was a constant underachiever, but all of a sudden, he found himself competing as a real contender in majors and advanced to the finals of the world's biggest tennis tournament, Wimbledon. What was different? Anyone who watched Nick play had an opinion about what came out of his mouth on court. He was constantly talking. In one instance he said to himself on court: "play FIFA 'til 3 am, what do you expect" when lamenting about his laziness. While a lot of his word vomits were super entertaining, very little of it was constructive. To me, it's not surprising at all that he often allows himself to say and THINK things that actually make him play worse! This is a guy who has gone on record so many times admitting that he hates tennis, hates competing, doesn't enjoy the grind, blah, blah, blah. Kyrgios realizes that he is super talented and really good at the sport of tennis, and while he wants to do well because it can bring him a lot of money and maybe fame, he isn't close to as competitive as any of the top players. He doesn't care enough to sacrifice much for enhanced success; he won't even drop the "I'm too cool" routine on court in order to bring him more wins! However, things changed last summer. Nick got a new girlfriend, and he literally credited her with keeping him "in line." I think it is possible that he felt a need to "do better" to possibly impress the new gf (a powerful motivational tool indeed!), and because of that, his enhanced competitiveness allowed him to improve his on court demeanor, and of course his self-talk became more constructive. It all came crashing down though in the 2022 Wimbledon final. Nick had played beautiful tennis all tournament, and was seemingly the better player for the early parts of the final. However, his lack of engrained competitive drive allowed his insecurities to surface, and out came the verbal rants. The match was in his hands after winning the first set 6-4 against Novak Djokovic, but Kyrgios wasn't mature enough to push the demons away and the match, and his shot at his first grand slam title, slipped away.

Another great example of the effect of self-talk comes from another of my favorite players, Ezra Loewy. Ezra is one of the smartest kids I have ever coached, but also one of the toughest for me to get through to. He is very stubborn, has a high achievement motivation, and is often very fearful of failure. A couple of years ago, we started our fall season of lessons off with a pretty significant adjustment with his backhand technique. While this was a pretty big change, I estimated the change would take at most a week or two to achieve a competent level. However, that is not exactly what happened. Ezra and I spent a lot of time working on this backhand, but so much of the time was spent with Ezra talking about how bad his backhand was, and how much worse it was from before. I worked hard to get him past this tough stage, but it just seemed that even when we made a step forward, we were taking two steps back. I definitely realized early how much his negative self-talk was hurting his chances at progressing and I shared this constantly with him, but Ezra just wasn't buying it. He was convinced that his reactions of exclaiming how bad he was were merely factual reports. After almost two months of extreme struggle, Ezra and I were both desperate for a solution. I asked Ezra how badly he wanted to escape this toil, and he confirmed the need to make it stop. That is when I came up with a bit of an extreme rule. I told Ezra that he simply wasn't allowed to say ONE negative thing about his backhand for the next seven days.

One week of preventing any negative self-talk is really tough to do, but as I said, Ezra was desperate, and because of that, he did it! He didn't say one negative thing about his backhand for one whole week! We had spent eight weeks working on this backhand. I, as a coach, was throwing out every coaching trick I could think of to make this backhand improve. Nothing worked until this one rule. After one week of zero negative comments about the backhand, he came to his Monday lesson and was actually ripping his backhand with confidence! He had reached an extremely competent level, and there honestly was no other reason other than the power of self-talk.

Mike concludes: I have sometimes been asked: do dramatic people feel worse? Worse is a word too subjective to address, but dramatic people do require more attention. Scientists have actually determined that there is a dramatic disorder called Histrionic Personality Disorder (HPD). Less than 2% of the population has HPD, so more than likely that particular dramatic person is just dramatic and not a sufferer of HPD. Every season I have a player that I think is dramatic. By dramatic, I mean a person who has to be the center of attention, a person who exaggerates all stories, a person who is demonstrative on the course, and a person who has a lot of negative self-talk. These players need a little more attention. I could ignore the behavior, but I have found this to be a mistake.

Dramatic players experience higher highs and lower lows. This is why they demand more attention, and that is okay. Lately, I have heard many conversations about keeping players level. The idea is that when a player's emotions are in check they will be more rational and make good game-time decisions. This makes perfect sense, but I don't believe it. I don't think that players are actually calm, cool and collected. One of my many favorite athletes is skier Bode Miller. As a skier I appreciate what he can do on course. Watching him on television, he seems so smooth and natural as he is going 90 mph down the mountain. Announcers constantly comment on how he is laid back and relaxed on skis. I'm not sure if it was a World Cup or an Olympic event, but the television coverage was monitoring Miller's heart rate. His face was very serene as he approached the starting gate, but as he got into position his heart rate spiked to nearly 200 bpm. Athletes are just ducks on a pond. On the surface they seem to glide around effortlessly, but really their legs are paddling so hard beneath the water's surface. Coaching a dramatic athlete takes more time, but it can also be easier. All of their emotions are above the surface. The Bode Millers of the world are the tough ones to coach.

I believe in using an athlete's so-called weaknesses as strengths. It may take more work and time, but that is what coaches and parents are supposed to do. There are times when a player may get too out of control, but there are warning signs that coaches and parents need to be aware of in order to stop the meltdown. A great way to stop a meltdown is to help the athlete paint a positive image in their head through self-talk, because ***a picture is worth a thousand words***.

A PICTURE IS WORTH A THOUSAND WORDS

*When I think about success I feel successful,
and when I feel like a success I act like a success.*

—Lainey Kathrein

A grad school thesis is often something that can be a bit of an overwhelming task. A student is supposed to take much of what they have learned as a graduate student and apply it to some sort of premise that they would like to prove and then share with the world. As a young impressionable student at Miami University in Oxford, Ohio, being the perfectionist that I was/am, I needed to find the perfect topic. I spent the first year of grad school racking my brain, stressing to find a topic. It just wasn't coming to me! At some point maybe I remembered the extremely important poster that was displayed on the wall of my Lexington High School English composition teacher's wall (Mrs. Wyatt): "writing the perfect paper is not possible," and so I relaxed and it sort of came to me. I was going to attempt to mesh what I had learned as a Sports Psychology graduate student with what I was learning as an assistant college coach into one PERFECT paper! Ha

The title of my thesis became *A Picture is Worth a Thousand Words*. The picture in reference here refers to a picture one can create in their own head. Visualization is one of the major concepts in Sport Psychology. It was certainly something I learned a great deal about in my classes at Miami University, but also something I became somewhat fascinated while watching and listening to other athletes.

As a child, visualization is called something much less scientific. That term is, of course, imagination. I remember vividly being on my driveway on Yorkshire Road, shooting around on my basketball hoop at the top of my garage. I was all by myself out there and maybe for a little while I was working on my shot mechanics or maybe it was my dribbling skills (or lack thereof), but the excitement of being out there shooting around on the court really started with "the game." There have been many commercials made emulating this game, and the ones in my driveway were no different. I would create a scenario such as this: my team is down 6 with a minute to go and then I would get a steal, take it quickly down the court and drive into the lane through traffic for a layup, but then I miss the shot but of course get my own rebound and put it back AND I get fouled! I make the free throw so now down just three points. Back on defense I block a shot off the backboard and then run down to the other end of the court to shoot a jumper that is just off the mark. I get my own rebound and then shoot a floater that bounces off the rim's front edge, and then I kick the ball out of bounds, so still down three. I then steal the inbounds pass with just seconds left, and shoot a tough leaner from deep; it goes IN! AND I get fouled!! OMG the crowd was going crazy! I go to the line with a second to go with a chance to win the game after being down six just seconds earlier, but miss the free throw! However, there is a lane violation on the other team and so I get to shoot another free throw and this one goes IN!! Game over!! World Champs!!

Now, I'm not sure how much of these sorts of "games" got lost in the age of video games and of course, likely diminished much further in this age of smartphones, but when I was a kid, imagination became an important trait to have while we created our own video games right outside our front doors!

Mike shares: The details of Jay's championship scenario are very impressive. Most of my championships just came with hitting one shot. The important aspect of visualization is desensitizing the athlete to stressful game situations. I know playing outside is a generational notion, but outside is where athletes grow. Athletes have to get off the couch (or gaming chair) and go play. Athletes need to play without structure. No structure means no AAU coaches, no MOJO coaches, no parents, just play and imagine success. Athletes are overloaded with structure to the point where they struggle to adapt and overcome game moments. An important aspect of creating scenarios is the athlete always makes the big play. In an earlier chapter we discussed the importance of confidence. Fictional scenarios aid in building an athlete's confidence. I hope in Jay's scenario he never misses that last shot (twice). Seriously Jay, a lane violation? In today's game we both know basketball officials swallow their whistles.

> **Jay shares further:** Spot on Mike - I was always a bit obsessed with making that last shot, and some of that *need* to be clutch actually was the cause of performance crippling anxiety. The worst of these moments came during the previously mentioned Lars Bleeker match. I wanted that win so badly, but I was not able to finish. I essentially missed "the last shot" multiple times and unfortunately, the lane violation couldn't help me. I lost the match and my overall psyche was actually dented so badly that it took over a year to mend.
>
> Six years later during my first year as a Sport Psychology graduate student, I went in to see Dr. Robin Vealey, one of the premier Sports Psychologists in the world and an advisor in my Miami U grad program, and I asked her about choking as I wanted to know how to prevent it. She profoundly stated to me that an athlete who is prepared physically, mentally and emotionally for any certain task at hand cannot choke. However, if an athlete is lacking in any one of those areas, then the stress of a certain situation could cause a negative performance, or

even a devastating choke. That made a lot of sense. Years later I connected a quote from Derrick Rose to this as he shared his 5 Ps in an interview. He said: *"proper preparation prevents poor performance."* This ideal became one of the foundations of my overall coaching skill set, and what I had learned from Dr. Vealey in that one statement helped me shape my thesis.

I was on a mission to figure out how to coach athletes in a way to at least greatly limit the chances of choking, if not prevent it completely. Later in my coaching career, this effort became a bit more positive oriented as I worked to develop skills of toughness as opposed to preventing weakness, but in my early 20s, the prevention of disaster was an important fear to overcome.

As the assistant tennis coach for the Miami University Women's team, I noticed early on that one of the major struggles the girls had was to play in matches at the same level they played in practice. Under the tutelage of head coach, Ray Reppert, these players began to practice so beautifully. Their level was extremely high, but for a lot of them, when they got in matches, their game sort of crumbled. I spent a lot of time with Karis Gibbs and Kelly Cook, two extremely talented players and two of the hardest working athletes I had ever been around. However, in matches, they almost tried TOO hard, and there were days where they looked like they almost forgot how to play! After one particularly tough day of matches, I went up to Coach Reppert and asked him how the girls could essentially lose the skills they developed in practice once we got into a match. He told me about the four levels of competence. He listed them as unconscious incompetence, conscious incompetence, conscious competence, and unconscious competence. He explained that there are players who do things wrong without understanding why, players who do things wrong but are aware of the cause of the mistake, players who do things right while thinking about producing the success, and finally, players who do things right without thinking at all. This last stage is what many coaches and sport psychologists call "the zone." I wanted to become a coach who could teach his athletes how to trigger this "zone!"

As I previously stated, writing a thesis can be tough, but being in the lab of the tennis courts each day certainly helped me build upon each set of thoughts I had. I wanted to help players play well in matches. A major question to answer was: what is so different in the match as opposed to practice? There are a lot of specific differences, but the one that stood out to me the most was speed. Now, I'm actually NOT talking about the speed of a ball or how fast someone can run; I'm talking about mental processing speed. Many athletes have spoken about a day of struggle as a day where the game was just going too fast. I've heard tennis players claim that the points and games just all happened in seconds after a collapse even though the collapse was almost 30 minutes long, whereas I've also heard baseball players say that a 95 mph fastball just seemed to be moving in slow motion right before belting it into the stands. I was realizing the great importance of the ability to process thoughts and produce skills at an efficient level. I was getting somewhere with this darn thesis! Now, how could I create greater processing speeds?

The answer was in the old cliché', "a picture is worth a thousand words." I theorized that if I could efficiently create positive pictures (or visualizations of positive performances) in the minds of my players, and if I could do so efficiently, it would be then that I could create an art of efficient learning while also creating the ability to trigger the production of successful actions.

Another of my favorite players at Miami was Kristen Baumgarner. Kristen had one of the most interesting struggles I have ever seen an athlete have. As a great tennis player and athlete, Kristen rarely could complete one of the easiest feats a tennis player has to execute. She could not toss the tennis ball for her serve. I would compare this to a basketball player not being able to dribble or a second baseman not being able to throw a ball to the first baseman (sorry Chuck Knoblauch!). When Kristen would begin her service motion and attempt to toss the ball up, it could go anywhere! She actually would often throw it up in the air 4-5 times and catch it the first four before finally hitting it the fifth time. It was agonizing to watch, and as her troubles with this continued, it actually became worse and worse. So, there we were in the basement of our University's basketball facility on a cold winter day, in a practice gym in Oxford, Ohio. Coach Reppert, Coach Dave Levy (who later in life became a "co-best man" at my wedding with my co-author here!), Kristen, and I were there to try and fix this tossing issue once and for all! After about an hour, nothing was working. Then, Kristen went to try and toss the ball again, and instead of tossing it softly above her head, she had what seemed to be some kind of seizure with her wrist as the ball darted behind all of us to the back wall with tremendous velocity. We all looked at each other stunned and then Kristen just broke down into tears. It was then that I somehow produced my first coaching stroke of genius!

Mike interrupts: Genius? Really?

Jay continues: Yes! Just listen!

As Kristen began to sob uncontrollably, I grabbed a ball, walked up to her and yelled: "KRISTEN! LOOK AT THIS! YOU SEE THIS BALL?" She then whimpered: "yeeees." I then exclaimed: "THROW IT RIGHT HERE! RIGHT HERE!" As I pointed to the exact spot in the air that we wanted her to throw this stupid toss, she whimpered, this time with a small amount of hope in her voice, "right there?" I sternly replied: "YES, RIGHT HERE!" As Kristen stepped up to attempt this, Ray and Dave looked at me like I was a complete moron! We all looked at each other and then back at Kristen and I believe we all thought that this stupid suggestion I made may just be crazy enough to work. As Kristen started her motion, I was SO nervous I could barely watch, but then IT happened. Kristen threw the perfect toss and then hit a great serve! We were ALL shocked, but then Ray cheered so loudly and then yelled: "DO IT AGAIN!" And so Kristen did toss it again and not only was that toss again perfect, she never had a tossing problem after that.

So one might ask what happened there. Kristen was in a state of extreme frustration that was causing her body and mind to seemingly lose connection. It also was causing her emotions to become out of control and I believe that when she released these emotions after the errant toss to the wall, she actually relaxed enough to allow an opening for her mind and body to connect again. When I stepped in to provide a quick and simple picture of the spot in the air to toss a ball to, her brain was able to create this picture, process it, and then her body produced a replication of that image. It was awesome! And the cool part of this was that I did it by saying just four words. THROW IT RIGHT THERE! Four words yielded a picture, and if a picture is worth a THOUSAND words, triggering it with just four seemed to be a pretty powerful and time efficient processing tool.

Being the perfectionist that I am, I wasn't satisfied with the 4 to 1000 ratio. I wanted it to be 1 to 1000. I wanted to develop in my players the ability to say just ONE word, and have that word trigger a clear picture that would have the power of 1000 words. This was a super fun task to accomplish in the labs of the Miami courts, and our players became super successful using them. These words mostly had to do with the triggering of proper stroke mechanics. For example, to make sure our #1 player, Kelly Squires, started her hand directly behind the ball and then brought her strings to the inside portion of the ball while finishing with a strong wrist to the left side of her left hip while hitting a slice backhand, we would remind her "inside." If she missed some and got confused at any time, we could say "inside" and she would produce the picture of doing things the right way. She could imagine herself in practice sharply hitting slice backhands into the corners. This was an extremely powerful tool to take into matches as it not only led to enhanced physical strokes and the strategic mental ability to quickly choose the correct shot for a certain moment, but it also created a great deal of emotional confidence. Dr. Vealey would be proud to hear how these methods have helped thousands of athletes I've coached over the years develop themselves into stronger competitors.

One of my very favorite students who was essentially obsessed with this overall process, is the late but great Gerald Ford. I started coaching Jerry as a 69-year-old, nine years ago. We nicknamed him "The President" for obvious reasons, and although he never actually held office in our White House, he was a man who loved to learn and tennis may have been his favorite hobby! I loved working with Jerry because he was the most engaged student I ever had. He would always book an hour court time before our lesson and about 10 minutes before I would walk out, I would see him go sit on the bench and go over his note cards. Yes, he took notes after all of our lessons! I would then come out and he would have 2-3 questions for me and most of the time, the questions referenced a lesson we had weeks earlier and something I had said that he wanted clarification on or help with. I needed to be sharp with this one, and I loved the challenge of that. A few months ago, just weeks before his passing at the age of 76 (too soon! ugh!), we had what may have been my favorite lesson of ours. Jerry had been playing better and more consistently than I had ever seen him play for weeks and he was still pushing to get more out of himself when he had a little epiphany. He realized that his past improvements had come because his informational processing speed had continuously improved on the court, and as we worked out, he pinpointed that for the next developmental steps to occur, he would need to choose trigger words (sound familiar?!) to allow him to transition from defensive areas of the court to the offensive areas with more efficiency and essentially with more calmness. I loved working with Jerry and loved him as a person because he taught me as much on the court as I taught him. I miss you Jerry!

Mike adds: Love the presidential story, Jay. Jerry was obviously a great man.

I am a big fan of the four levels of competence. The fourth level is very similar to flow state. One of my favorite pastimes is reading about flow states ("the zone"). Gio Valiante published a great book on golf flow states. One of the more intriguing aspects of flow states is time. An athlete in a flow state loses the concept of time. During the Covid shut down my daughter and I had to search hard to find an open golf course. We found one about an hour away in Medina, Ohio, called Shale Creek. It was early Spring so the course was a little soggy and the air was brisk. Neither Alaina or I expected much out of the round, as it was just good to get out.

Alaina got off to a pretty good start. She was hitting fairways, but with the wet conditions, she wasn't getting the roll she needed to have good approach shots. She was having to hit long irons and hybrids into the greens. Often she was coming up a little short, but her short game was pretty solid. She finished the first nine with a 39. We grabbed a snack and moved to the second nine. I won't go into a hole by hole account of the second nine, but she did shoot a 32. She finished the round with a one under 71 (a personal best). As her dad I loved the score, but as her coach I loved what she said to me on the 18th tee box. She and I have a rule about never discussing scores during a round. All I said to her on the tee box was that we had one more hole to go. She replied, "wait this is it?" I of course responded with an affirmative answer.

Alaina had completely lost track of time and place. It was the ultimate flow state … a flow state that athletes strive to get into but seldom do. On the second nine she and I never talked about golf. We simply hit shots and talked about whatever came to our minds. She never asked for club selection or course management tips; she simply played golf. Now, the million-dollar question (or whatever number sport psychologists charge their professional clients) is how does an athlete get into a flow state on command?

Jay concludes: The exact trigger into the flow state WOULD be worth about a million dollars! In my opinion, the power of visualization cannot be overstated as an important variable in the search for the flow state, or "zone" as many call it, and this has been evident to me on so many occasions, so I wanted to share one more example here.

In 1996, as I started as the head coach at Bowling Green, Radu Bartan was my #1 player. Radu grew up in Romania, and he was an extremely hard-working and driven individual. Realizing the importance of the serve in regards to his success, Radu came up to me after practice one day to ask if he could hit 1000 serves after practice and also if he could do that every day. As I quickly said yes, I was trying to imagine how long it would take Radu to hit these 1000 serves. Well, the answer is about two hours! So for the next month, every day after our 2-2.5 hour practice, Radu would hit serves for another two hours. It was wildly impressive to me, and his serve did get a lot better. However, a month later, he came to me and told me that because of all the time serving, he was starting to struggle academically. I then came up with some more coaching genius: I said, "Radu, how about you try this? How about you change your serving plan? Instead of hitting 1000 serves a day, you will hit just 333 serves per day. The difference though is that before every serve, you will visualize the motion and the serve going in perfectly, and you will repeat that image production after every serve. If you do this 333 times, then in your mind, you will have actually hit 999 serves. Then at some point before you get back into your dorm room I want you to think of one more great serve as you always have to make your last shot, and this last shot will be #1000." Not only did Radu save hours of time to be able to gear towards academic success, but his serve actually developed at a faster rate and quickly became a consistent weapon!

BEING A PERFORMER

*Having a vision or a plan is just the start;
success depends on execution.*

—Michael Kathrein

Jay begins the performance: I have loved sports for as long as I can remember, and I've admired athletes from all kinds of sports throughout. When thinking about why I revere these men and women, and especially when thinking of the ones I gravitate toward the most, I quickly realize it's the true performers who catch my eye. It's the athletes who not only seem to love to be on the biggest stages, but those who somehow produce their highest level performances when the most people are watching. The Tiger Woods chip in on the 16th at the 2005 Masters comes to mind; the Michael Jordan slight push-off and dagger to take the 1998 NBA championship is an incredible moment in time; Kirk Gibson's walk off home run in game one of the 1988 World Series was truly iconic. There have been times when watching a game end with such a clutch shot, that I've almost felt like I was watching an actor perform in a movie. It was as if I expected David Tyree to catch that ball off his helmet in Super Bowl XLII, and then as if the script had already been written, for Eli Manning to continue to lead his Giants the rest of the way down the field for the winning TD.

As coaches, we have all coached players who have struggled to take the high-leveled performance in practice into the game or match. It's an age-old dilemma for players and coaches everywhere. What can be done to help an athlete take their "A-game" into the real competition, and then to take it to the next level? How can an athlete be trained to produce levels in the most important moments that may be higher than they've ever achieved?

The first step here is to work to understand the athlete we are working with. When I first came to New York to coach in the McEnroe Academy, I worked with a teenaged Noah Rubin. Noah was the type of athlete who LOVED the stage. It was actually hard to get him to practice with a high level of emotional intensity because he felt like he would save that for the matches. Now, he worked hard physically and was almost always very focused in these training sessions, but when he walked between the lines in competition, Noah was different. The adrenaline kicked in and not only did he go in with the intent to battle from beginning to end, he loved every second and every aspect of that battle. Noah loved these battles so much that it led him to a Junior Singles Wimbledon Title, and a chance later in his career to battle with none other than Roger Federer at the Australian Open. Unfortunately for Noah, Roger MAY have had a greater love for the big stage than almost anyone in any sport ever.

In my sporting experiences, Noah is an outlier. Most of my players and students in many sports find their best performances coming in their practices, and will almost beg and plead to figure out how to bring that out when the bright lights come on. Most coaches have had players "freeze" during competition, and others have just seen them play at a level much lower than they are capable of, or at least lower than had been witnessed in practice. Many of these players look around at their surroundings a lot during play. They often look at their parents, maybe hoping for a sense of appraisal, but usually worrying about how the possible disapproval will later be shared with them. As a college coach, the parental issue wasn't something we had to deal much with because of the separation between our athletes and their parents (some of the parents were literally a half a world away!), but wow, coaching junior players (high schoolers and younger) is much different indeed! Parents at our Tennis Academy sit right on the court during private lessons and often watch the entirety of training sessions, so one can imagine how involved they are during the competitions! The parents often become untrained coaches and sports psychologists, and they may not understand how damaging the immediate replay of their child's performance during the car ride home could be. I recently had a player who was really self-aware, and not only did he realize how poorly he played when his parents came to watch, but he actually understood the psychology holding him down. In one particular parent post-match rant, this player of mine had lost trust with his dad because his dad's judgements of the match were just so outlandish. To his credit, Julian had the guts to go to his parents and ask them not to come to any more matches. And to their credit, they agreed to the wishes and Julian's performances began to immediately improve. Now, for me, this was all okay, but not ideal. I told Julian that I wanted to set a goal with him, that he would work to become such a tough performer, and also a good "translator," that he would be able to invite his parents back to watch him compete. A year later, he did just that! To accomplish this, he had to learn to keep his focus on the task at hand while pushing away distractions; he had to be ready to take on all sorts of verbal feedback during and after matches, and importantly, he needed to learn how to let the "fans" inspire greater performances.

Many parents can bring themselves in line before creating this level of emotional baggage, but some definitely need to be helped. I often share one of my favorite "parent training" pieces, and that comes from a Bruce Brown and Robert Miller article, *"What Makes A Nightmare Sports Parent – And What Makes A Great One."* Here, hundreds of athletes explained the damaging effects of "the ride home," while the same athletes were asked what triggered the times they felt great about their parents' feedback, and the "overwhelming response" was that their parents had simply said: "I love to watch you play." Those six understated words are so incredibly powerful that I feel they cannot be shared enough.

I've encouraged and implored countless parents of players and even my own sister (an intensely competitive parent herself!) to use these words. I've even prohibited certain parents from saying anything but these words for 24 hours after a match!

While making sure the parental factor remains helpful, or at least not a deterrent towards peak performance, there is much more work to be done in order to transform an athlete into a true performer. The first for me is to get the athlete to connect with the possible adrenaline boosters around. These could come from various things of course. For example, a Broadway performer gets on stage and undoubtedly derives a great amount of energy from the crowd. While the fact that there are hundreds of fans hanging on every word said could create stage fright, for the world's greatest performers, they simply make a different "choice." Yes, every performer has a choice. They can choose to imagine the embarrassment that losing could cause, OR they can choose to visualize the crowd's jubilation when their performance reaches all new levels.

Last summer, at the age of 51, I was asked to play in a National Basketball Tournament in NYC. This was part of the UHoops League that I play in at my Lifetime Club here on Long Island, and even though I am old, I was asked to fill a roster spot on our Open Team for the tourney. Now, I didn't get much playing time to be honest, BUT I was put in during our quarterfinal game with about 10 minutes to play, and because my level remained super solid, I was left in even in the waning minutes of a fairly tight game. After our opponents hit a three to cut our lead to just three points with about 15 seconds left, I was fouled and put on the line to shoot a one and one. I knew that making this first free throw would cement the win for us, but I also knew that if I missed, our opponents would have a chance to tie with another three-pointer. I also knew that if I missed, my teammates, young peers of mine, would view me with a bit less respect. The thought of that bothered me. So, I went to the line and I made some choices.

The first was to realize that the aforementioned negative thoughts needed to leave my brain almost immediately! I had to push them aside. The second was to choose to replace those thoughts with other thoughts, knowing that if I didn't fill my brain with something productive, the negative thoughts would surely return. As I was given the basketball at the foul line, I looked over to my bench. I saw my coach filming on his iPhone (immediately dismissing the thought of what a miss would look like on film), and I saw my teammates seemingly on the edge of their seats on the bench. I chose to allow this to excite me. I then visualized them cheering loudly when I made the shot and took this emotion into my pre-shot ritual. I followed the ritual, first reminding myself that I have done this a million times and then saying "stay tall" which helps me finish the stroke better and create more arc, all the while feeling the emotional expectation of happiness coming from the cheers of my teammates. I took the shot, swished it, and they cheered, just as expected. I then swished the second for good measure, just to make sure everyone realized the first wasn't a fluke. Motivation is important, but feeling the right emotion is key to creating the best performances.

Mike joins the stage: I am certainly glad Jay made his free throws. That goes down as one of the greatest sports stories of all time. Forget about the alley-oop from Dereck Whittenburg to Lorenzo Charles to win the 1983 National Championship. Forget about Christian Laettner's shot to beat the Wildcats in 1993. Forget about Auburn returning a missed field goal for the game winning touchdown in the 2016 SEC Championship. Jay Harris's recreation league free throws are legendary. I am only slightly joking. Of course since it is Jay I have to make fun of him a little, but Jay did what performers do – they execute. Very few athletes will ever have a stage like Charles, Laettner, or the Auburn football team. So athletes have to value the stage they do have, even if it is the New York City Recreation League at age 51. What Jay did so well is put things in the right perspective.

He immediately removed the negative consequences of the moment and visualized the positives.

I have coached a number of practice range studs. These are the players that hit great shots at the range but were rather pedestrian on the golf course. Several athletes fail to have their shot making skills at the practice range translate to the golf course. To help athletes be performers, I encourage them to create the stage and scenarios during practice sessions that are required during competition. This will help normalize the actual stage. A player can never fully create a stage in practice, but visualizing success in practice helps tremendously. Practice sessions don't have the adrenaline of game time performances, as they don't have the fans, nor do they have parents (most of the time).

> **Jay concludes the performance:** Practice may not have the fans. My recreation league/NATIONAL tournament (ha) may not have a real crowd, BUT that doesn't mean a coach or a player can't create adrenaline! My heart was racing a mile a minute as I approached the line in that game. Why? Because I cared. And THAT is key. When Noah Rubin was emotionless during certain practices, I pleaded with him to realize that if he could bring some emotion to his practices, he would be able to handle them better in matches. And when another of my favorite students, former Georgia Tech legend and current Florida State star Gabriele Brancatelli, was wearing his emotions on his sleeve showing how much he cared, I worked to teach him skills to keep him calm enough to enjoy the excitement of the tennis stages he involved himself in so that he could produce peak performances.
>
> Mike talks here about the creation of a "stage" during practices. This is incredibly important! A great coach can create a sense of pressure during practice that can mirror the pressure an athlete will feel during the game. However, a truly great competitor will individually do this during practice, and THAT is far more powerful than any situation a coach can create. Jordan

may very well be the GOAT of all basketball players, but that can be debated. What can't be debated in my opinion is that the greatest internal pressure producer in any sport is also Michael Jordan. Jordan could create adrenaline with a snap of the finger any time he wanted. It could be during the practice where he battled so hard with the "super athletic" Steve Kerr that he ended up punching him in the face, or it could be during a somewhat meaningless regular season game where he made up a story that the guy guarding him talked shit about him to the papers. For those millennials, the "papers" refers to the newspaper reporters.

How do the best competitors create the best performances? My best explanation is that they are willing to seek people to perform FOR instead of looking for people they can let down. These people could be guys on a rec league basketball bench; they could be the millions of cursed yet exceptionally loyal Cleveland fans praying for a championship before they die; or they could be the parents we all want to please. The best performers simply go out there with a mindset that it doesn't matter what adversity presents itself because it's all about taking an approach that the only important thing is to fight through the next moment in front of them. There is no fear of embarrassment. There is no fear of losing. There is only the desire to perform, and for the most extreme competitors, the desire is to perform better than anyone alive.

PART THREE: CHARACTER

Simply put, sports build character. Character is essentially the summary of one's qualities, and the strength of these qualities are what allows a person to be successful in tackling certain challenges. Those stronger athletes possess incredible composure and realize that where they were in the past isn't what is important; it's who they are now and who they want to become in the future that defines the ultimate quality of their character.

Here in GAME SET LIFE, we do not shy away from the realization that there are plenty of ups and downs during any one competition and even more in long seasons, and we also understand how all of this mirrors the high and low points in life. Coaches everywhere work to find players who model tremendous focus, coachability, and intense work ethic, as it is these players who become the leaders in the clubhouse.

We have both been lucky enough to coach a lot of these sorts of leaders, and we have been equally lucky enough to watch them find career success after hanging up their racquets, clubs, cleats etc. As one can guess, CHARACTER shown not only impacted their success in competition, it also impacted all those around them, including us as coaches! These leaders at times taught us coaches as much if not more than we taught them, and that is honestly the true value of sitting in what a good friend of mine once called, "the toy store of life", which is the position of coaching teams and programs.

In this third section, we realize "there is always more to give" and we work to help parents, coaches and athletes push the right buttons in order to help all build CHARACTER as it is the most important aspect of any scoreboard in LIFE.

STOPLIGHT METHOD

Champions keep playing until they get it right.
Then they play more.

—Billie Jean King

As a first year head college coach in the "metropolis" of Bowling Green, Ohio, on land where the highest point in the entire county was a man-made hill built on the University golf course, I coached an incredibly driven young man by the name of David Anderton. Dave was originally from Canada, and he was entering his junior year when I arrived. I immediately noticed that Dave was the best athlete on our entire team, but when I also noticed his high-risk playing style, I was a bit confused. I also became confused when I learned that Dave was an emotional fella, a guy who struggled to control his anxiety. All of that to me just seemed to go together about as well as oil and water, or plaid on the east coast (sorry Mike, had to throw that in there! ha).

For David Anderton to become a successful tennis player, I believed something needed to change. He was essentially wasting his athleticism by playing a style that created quick points, and his lack of control for his nerves didn't vibe so well with the risky play either, especially in the big moments of matches. So, the first thing we did was to change his entire game style. Many may think it to be crazy for a first year, 24-year old head coach to attempt such a feat, and many may also have found Dave a bit crazy to go along with this idea, but to his credit, he soaked it in like a sponge, and he began playing a slower, more grinding style of tennis where his points, and matches, became longer, and he started to realize how his athleticism was helping him to win, sometimes even more than his tennis skill. He had some solid wins in the fall playing mostly #5 & 6 in our line-up, and when the fall season ended, he was happy, but not content. That is when things got super interesting.

Dave went home to Canada for the winter break, and there, he and his best friend, Joey Scrivano (current head women's coach at Baylor University), decided to take certain aspects of their games to the extreme. Joey was also a junior at the time, playing for Eastern Michigan University, and he was having some of the same mental issues that Dave was having. So, they both decided to dedicate an entire month of practice on rituals. For the first week, they actually did not hit one ball! They went on the court each day for an hour-long practice, and they pretended to play points. After each "point," they both focused intensely on their rituals. What I mean by this, is that they wanted to create physical habits that led to mental stability. They were going to practice these physical actions in between points, as they felt that those may be even MORE important than the physical actions they created during the points. Dave and Joey both began behaving almost robotic after each of these fake "points." Dave, for example, would walk to the same areas of the court; he would make the same gestures; he would hold his racquet the same exact way and even work to walk at the same pace. After a week of doing this without hitting a ball, Dave and Joey added the balls back in, and practiced for another 3-4 weeks, still focusing mostly on the rituals, in preparation for the winter/spring season, which is the main season for college tennis.

When Dave got back to Bowling Green in January, he was a different person. It was truly amazing the transformation that he went through! His emotions seemed completely controlled on court, and because of that, his results were immediately impressive. They were so impressive, that within three weeks, Dave went from #6 in our line-up to #2! He was simply winning at every spot we put him in. The tactical rituals had helped him feel so controlled on court, that his confidence to seemingly accomplish anything he wanted was soaring. It would be like taking 10-pound ankle weights off of a runner, and then letting him compete against the same runners he was almost beating before. Dave had essentially removed the 10 pound weights that were holding him back mentally, and now he was just enjoying running free again! Dave's career success was enhanced incredibly because of his diligence in working with rituals, and I know that it is something he coaches to this day. Dave later became a college coach himself; at one point he was named the National Assistant Coach of the Year and is currently enjoying his 23rd year as a college coach.

One of the great things about being a college coach is that one gets to learn from his players. Dave taught me a lot in just the two years I had the privilege of coaching him, and the amazing effect a mastery of rituals can have on a person was just one of them. From those learnings, I started to develop what I now call the *Stoplight Method*.

The premise behind the Stoplight Method is pretty easy to figure out in terms of what the colors signify, and I will explain how they relate to an athlete on a field, court or course.

As many may know, tennis players are allowed to take a maximum of 20 seconds in between points. Very few take anywhere close to that length of time on court, but interestingly, in recent years, one of the best players of all time, Rafael Nadal, has received a lot of criticism for his use (or abuse as some claim) of this time period. A beginning player may wonder why one would need to take that much time in between points. It only takes a few seconds to collect the balls after a point concludes (obviously zero time for the pros when they have ball kids!) and then a few seconds to step up to the line and serve. So what takes so long? What happens in those 15-20 seconds? Is it necessary to take all that time? The answer is yes and no, and THAT is where the Stoplight Method comes in.

I suppose it's important to first identify the colors of the stoplight...

Mike quips: I think they probably know that!

Jay continues: Yes, I realize, but just to make sure—there are of course three colors on a stoplight and in teaching my athletes how to use the Stoplight Method, I get them to sort of view themselves as cars. When the light is green (meaning everything is going great), they should keep driving the car on to the next point at the same speed, no need to slow down or speed up significantly. When the light is yellow (meaning they may have hit a couple of obstacles or aren't feeling great), that's time to slow down a bit, be a little cautious, think a bit more about the surroundings and goings on.

Mike adds: Jay was training to drive in NYC his whole life. He's the world's worst driver. He was a distracted driver before that was a thing. If a person was taught what not to do as a driver, it was because Jay did that very stupid thing behind the wheel like passing people on the shoulder, driving at least 20 mph over the speed limit, steering with his knees because one hand was on his phone and the other was holding a Coke, taking half of the road as he drove down the middle, never using his directional signal, and setting the world record for rolling through stop signs.

Jay continues: I never have claimed to always have practiced what I've preached! And I do have a great story about rolling through a stop sign and getting stopped in Cincinnati (full details in *THE REAL COLLEGE ATHLETES*). The policeman pulled me out of the car and asked me that if he started hitting me over the head with his flashlight, would I like him to stop or just slow down. I understood his point!

The last color, when the light is red (meaning significant frustrations or anxiety have been produced or a tough match obstacle has presented itself), then I would want my athlete to take a lot more time before returning to the next live action, kind of like sitting (and stopping) at a red light!

I often tell a story about a match I played just about six years ago to illustrate the dos and don'ts of this method. I was playing in the News Journal Tennis Tournament in my hometown of Lexington, Ohio for the third time in my 40s (during a "career comeback" of sorts). I had first played in the NJ Tourney at the age of 11 as I captured the Boy's 12 & under title that year after a huge 6-4, 6-0 win over Doug Hartzler in the final. And yes, I do remember the scores of all my matches in that event, and almost all tennis events I've been a part of! After winning multiple junior titles (10), I went on to win the men's open singles event six times, with the last coming in 2002, as a 30-year old. Having made the semifinals in my first return to the NJ as a 40-year old, I still felt I could do better, and a part of me was loving the idea of possibly winning this event in my teens, 20s, 30s and now 40s! So, I entered the 2015 NJ as the 4th seed (which may have actually been a little generous). I played well in the early rounds and advanced to the semifinals fairly unscathed. I learned that when playing tournaments at this age, one must almost pray not to induce a calf strain, stomach pull, slipped disc in the back, or some other injury that would essentially stop the train in its tracks. I was excited to take on Alex "Bones" McCann in the semis match-up, but also pretty nervous. I've played this tournament for so long and it means so much to me that I really just always want to show a great effort AND produce a respectable performance. Alex was a recent college graduate for a nationally ranked Middle Tennessee State program where he played alongside Jon Peers, a two-time grand slam doubles champion. I feared that Alex had the ability to not only negate any "great effort" I could produce, but that he also had the ability to embarrass me on the court. Nonetheless, I walked onto the court with a pretty good game plan and some healthy confidence. That combination proved to be lethal for about 90 minutes and I found myself up 6-2, 4-0. The green Stoplight was beaming the entire time, and I was rolling. That's when "it" happened. At 6-2, 4-0, I was about to start the next serving game. I had been serving incredibly well and Alex was honestly a mess. His knuckles were bleeding from punching his strings (yes tennis players are so weird!) and he had all but thrown in the towel. At that moment, my thoughts wandered to something else though. As much as I've benefited in my tennis career from being highly analytical, sometimes it can be a burden. At that moment, I CHOSE to realize that if I lost that serving game (on the good side in terms of the sun/wind) and then Alex held serve, I would be faced with the challenge of serving into the sun and if I got broken there and then Alex held again, the score would be 4-4. What?! How could I be in this "precarious situation" after playing as close to perfect as I've ever played for the entire match up to that point? I couldn't shake that feeling, but still chose to step up to serve. I double faulted, my first of the match. I then double faulted again, love-30. I immediately feared that I had given Alex some hope, but I looked over at him and he really didn't look so hopeful. So I played another few points pretty quickly and fought back to deuce. However, my mind (and body) had become so tightly wound that I could barely swing my racquet. I double faulted twice in a row to give away the game. Alex then held the next game to make it 2-4. Now I was going to be serving into the sun. I knew this game would be tough. I was still super tight, and now Alex felt a bit hopeful for a chance to crawl right back into the match. While I had obviously thwarted any chance of being embarrassed by being blown out, choking a 6-2, 4-0 lead would likely be a more embarrassing loss than I've ever had, especially with the mental "skills" that I believe to be in possession of! I slowed down a bit in that game. I essentially noticed the yellow light, and took some time; I gutted out a tough game to take a 5-2 lead. I just needed to win four more points... not so tough, right? Well, I allowed Alex to hold at love as he was pushing me around like a little sister (that's a reference to MY sister, Nickie, not the gender so relax!). I would now be serving on the good side with a 5-3 lead, just a couple of good serves away from closing out what would be one of my top five wins of my entire tennis career. Then "it" happened again. I played that game like I was driving on the Audubon. Not once did I stop to make a plan. Not once did I slow down to emotionally prepare myself for any sense of a peak performance state. I got broken. The score was now 5-4 and Alex was set to serve back on the good side after the changeover. I was letting this opportunity slip away.

A tennis fan knows that after every odd game, the players switch sides. During this changeover, the players have some extra time to sit, think, towel off, re-hydrate, or in my case at that moment, lament solely about how someone of my apparent mental ability could have allowed this mental collapse. That internal conversation wasn't so helpful either. So, I got ready to play the next point; I lost it. I then lost the next point, 30-love Alex. He was just two points from inexplicably tying the score in the second set. All of a sudden, a lightbulb went off! And it was red!! I took some extra time after that point, possibly Nadal-like extra time. I walked back to the back corner of the court by the fence, looked through the fence at the grass growing, and I took a DEEP breath. I then thought about the score, 6-2, 5-4, 30-0, and thought that if I could somehow tough out this game, it would create an incredibly proud moment. I also thought about the style and structure of play I had used to build my 6-4, 4-0 lead and realized that I hadn't executed or even attempted anything close to that in about 30 minutes. I turned back to the court knowing that I had shown some extreme toughness on this very court SO many times in my life. I was now excited for this challenge and was focused on the exact structure I would build in this next point. I played two of the most impressive points I've ever played in my life to get the score to 30-30, two points from the win. I was playing another great point when Alex hit a very unexpected flat down the line backhand. I stretched to my limit and returned a slice backhand floater as he approached the net, and thank goodness, missed a sitter volley to give me match point. I was very relieved but honestly felt deserved of that point. I didn't believe he was going to execute both the amazing backhand AND the volley; at least that's how I got myself to feel. One more point to go; I needed to execute the same structure again. I felt great. Big serve coming I knew. He missed his first serve. I immediately got super nervous. No time for a red light stop now. He was going to hit a second serve in about four seconds. I needed to be ready. But I'm supposed to win this point now. It would be embarrassing not to win it. Gotta push that line of thinking away now! Okay, done. Focus on the structure. I'm ready. I'm going to rip this return to his backhand side to get in the pattern I want. I'm ready. He serves. It catches the net. Match over! I've won! And I deserved that double fault for pushing through all of that torture and truly being ready to play that match point, or so I got myself to believe…

Mike reacts: Isn't there a children's game called *Red Light, Green Light*? It is an interesting approach to find an appropriate level of emotions. I am finding that younger players need to find more emotion. John McEnroe played with a great deal of emotion (some of it staged), and other athletes played with no outward emotion. What is the perfect amount?

Jay answers: "*You cannot be serious!*" This is likely Johnny Mac's most famous line, but yes, he had many such outbursts. Were some of them staged? You're damn right they were staged! Johnny is easily one of the most competitive athletes ever. He hates to lose (which he expressed in detail as he prepared for the recent Pickleball Slam!), and while on tour, would do anything to put himself in a position to win. He used many tactical strategies to help him win, but he also manipulated his own emotions. While some of his outbursts and confrontations with officials were completely genuine, others were attempts to either get himself to perform at a higher level, or to get under his opponents' skin a bit in order to bring his level down. He was recently quoted in an interview with Henrik Lundquist when asked when he played his best: "I'm not sure I was ever calm, but believe it or not, to me, I was always under control. I took it to the limit. I could push it and get a little louder to sort of get things going." While these methods helped McEnroe win seven grand slam tournaments, many would claim that if he could have controlled these emotional eruptions, he would have won far more. It is also possible, in my opinion, that if he was able to feel less stressed on court emotionally while he was on the tour, he may have not experienced the desire to quit the tour in the middle of his playing career. While he did come back after his hiatus, Mac (similar to Jordan) would have almost certainly won more titles had he not had that time away.

Mike, I'm not sure there is a perfect level of emotional expression an athlete should have, especially given the fact that the mental build for all athletes is different; however, my rule here is very simple. An athlete (and the coach!) need to find the emotional level where peak performance occurs, and when this happens, the path to that level needs to be quickly figured out. For some, this could be a level that is more hyped and for others, the right level could be something much more serene. Once this is identified, the mechanisms taking the athlete towards a euphoric state and/or away from an anxious or frustrated state should be continuously practiced.

Mike concludes: I think it is time for another Michael Jordan anecdote. When you are the greatest player on the planet how do you get motivated to play Puerto Rico? This was a conundrum of Michael Jordan in the summer of 1992. The real "Dream Team" was assembled to dominate the Olympic Games. The "Dream Team" had some preliminary games in the United States. One of these games was in Portland, Oregon, against Puerto Rico. The reason I refer to this team as the real "Dream Team" is the fact that they won every game by an average of over 40 points. So, I repeat the question, how does Jordan get motivated? Jordan's teammate, Charles Barkley, shared this story and it is one of my favorites.

"So we're playing in Portland, Oregon, in the tournament of the Americas. So me, Chuck Daily, David Robinson and Michael [Jordan] go out and play [golf] in the morning of the game. We're not playing till like eight o'clock at night. We play 18 and Chuck says 'ok, that was a great time'. Michael says 'I'm playing another 18!' We're like 'Michael, we got a game tonight.' He's like 'Chuck, I'll be fine, blah blah blah'.

So Michael comes back after playing another 18, we're getting ready for the game. Chuck [Daily] says 'Hey Charles, you got this guy, Patrick or David, whoever started that night, Scottie you got this guy...' and then Michael says 'No, I got him!' It was the point guard from Puerto Rico, and Chuck says 'Well he's the point guard, Michael'. Michael looks at him and says 'I said I got him! I read something he said about me in the newspaper, and I got him.' And the whole room's like 'Dude you just played 36 holes of golf' and Coach says 'and you gonna guard the point guard?!'

Michael would not let this little dude dribble. He's talking to him. You know that stupid drill when you try to turn guys and you're like 'yo, you can't go, turn the other way?!' Michael had played 36 holes of golf and he's talking to this guy the whole time. 'Hey don't you ever talk about me publicly again! I'm Michael Jordan! Don't you ever talk about me!'"

Barkley thought Jordan was crazy. Jordan's competitiveness is legendary and there are many stories out there about it. Barkley thought there was something wrong with Jordan. It was just the opposite, Charles. Jordan was creating the level of emotion needed in a game against a far inferior opponent. How many times has the better team struggled because they played down to the level of competition? There was no chance of this happening with Jordan on the team. When the greatest player on the planet puts forth that effort, his teammates are then inspired to match that level of intensity. Jordan not only created the emotion he needed, but also provided emotion for his team. Jordan created that picture that was worth a thousand words of inspiration. He chose to make a villain out of the Puerto Rican player. I'm guessing Jordan probably doesn't remember that particular player's name indicating he wasn't a villain. We always remember a villain's name. To generate the proper emotion, a player often must create a villain. Michael Jordan created a passion or certain energy level to compete against an inferior opponent. After playing golf all morning (and I'm sure he was drinking Gatorade), it would be very easy to be complacent. Using *A Picture is Worth a Thousand Words*, a player can create the energy needed to not only be competitive, but dominant. Circling back to "You cannot be serious!" could one missed call (allegedly) really send a professional tennis player into a tirade? Or, was he doing that to create the correct emotional state to win? Some athletes are stoic and focus on remaining calm. They believe this helps keep their minds clear from passion and they are likely to make good game-time decisions. Yet, other athletes thrive on playing with emotion. They need the fire. It's the old cliché', know thyself!

THE MASTER TRANSLATORS

Whoa to the makers of literal translations, who by rendering every word weaken the meaning!

— Voltaire

As a high school junior I was playing in the finals of my conference tennis tournament at the number one singles spot. I was playing against an old rival, RC Speck, a good friend of mine. RC had beaten me a good amount early in my playing days, but I hadn't even lost a set to him for about four years. I was the favorite going into the match for sure, but RC was a very talented player and always a dangerous opponent. I came out in the first set of the match probably nervous to lose, and RC came out guns blazing. He won the first set 6-2, and then broke my serve in the first game of the second to go up 1-0. Now, a quick backstory: this was a big match for me for a few reasons. The biggest reason was that my dad, my coach, hadn't decided yet if I would be playing singles or doubles in the state qualifier tournaments. I had played doubles my first two years of high school, and felt very ready to play singles in this, my junior year. However, coach had not been convinced yet, and I knew a loss on this day could push him towards making me play doubles. Not only did I want to play singles for my own selfish reasons of showing that I could do it on the singles court, but I also knew that if I played doubles, I would play with a teammate that I wasn't necessarily getting along with at the time. So, losing the first set and getting down an early break in the second was NOT the start I was looking for on this particular day. Then, my dad walked over to my court for the first time in the match. Uh oh, who knew what he was about to say to me at this moment, but I knew it wasn't going to be pleasant. However, because of some past "self-training," I knew I had to be ready to translate it into something constructive.

Two years earlier, I was a freshman playing in my first high school singles match. I was excited to be in the singles lineup after having played just doubles prior to that, and I felt like I was playing pretty well ... maybe not perfect but I was displaying some really good stuff. My dad walked over to the fence at one point and motioned me over. I sheepishly walked to the fence and he sternly said to me: "Jay. Not only are you an embarrassment to yourself out on that court right now, you're an embarrassment to me, an embarrassment to your whole family and definitely an embarrassment to your team, to your school and really the entire town!! Now, if you don't pick it the f' up, then I'm gonna come out there and rip your ass off the court." I quickly replied: "But dad, I'm up 5-2." He immediately barked back: "And that's why you'll never be a good tennis player!" And then he walked away. Those types of conversations were fairly common during my first two years of high school on the tennis team with my dad as my coach. During my freshman year, I lost only three matches the entire season, but I cried after six! Obviously I wasn't so good at handling these sorts of conversations, mostly because I simply wasn't equipped with any real mental skills to do so. However, maybe in an act of survival, I knew I had to develop some. I knew my dad loved me and I had no doubt that his entire goal was for me to do well. I also knew and realized there was some genius behind his messages as he simply looked to push whatever button he could in order to get me to play better. I had seen him do it for years on the basketball court. Now, I'll say that not all the buttons were successful, but I realized at some point that it wasn't just him pushing the buttons. I was just as responsible to learn how to receive certain messages and use that to push my own buttons.

So, when my dad walked out onto that court with me down to RC 6-2, 1-0, the skills I had developed were ready for the challenge.

As he approached me, he was already muttering something about how on most days he was very happy that he had a son. When he got to me, he looked right at me and said: "Today is not one of those days." As if that wasn't enough, he continued. He said something to me that sparked the competitiveness in my brain. He said: "Well, I guess you're playing doubles in the state qualifier," and then he walked away. I learned by then not to respond but instead just to absorb. If that comment would've been made to me my freshman year, before I became what I would call a "master translator," I might've crumbled. I might've said to myself, "Oh my god, I'm going to have to play doubles and I bet he's already made up his mind." But instead, I said to myself "Alright Jay, enough is enough! It's time to play some inspired tennis because there is no way I am losing to RC Speck and there is no way I'm playing doubles in the state qualifiers!" Now, my dad didn't say any of those words, but those are the only words I heard and those are the words that I used to get myself back on track. I won that match 2-6, 6-2, 6-1. After the last point, my good friend RC came up to shake hands and he asked me what my dad said in that very quick conversation that we had at 6-2, 1-0. He was like: "Jay! He came out on the court, said like four words, and then all of a sudden you were a completely different guy! Like, what the hell?! What did he say to you?!" I laughed and just told him that he told me to move my feet more. RC said: "Jay come on! No way! What did he say?" I told him that my dad told me that if I lost or if I kept playing the way I was then I was gonna have to play doubles with Sivram in the states. We both laughed a little bit and while RC thought that a simple threat was all it took to get me inspired, I knew that it was a lot deeper than that.

Mike interjects: Jay's dad (John) and I have a lot in common. We both are, or in John's case, were teachers at Lexington High School. We both have coached a bunch of different sports, both boys and girls. We both have coached our daughters at high levels. We are both avid golfers, Browns fans, and Buckeye fans. We both hate to lose, and most importantly we both know how to fire up Jay. Coaching your kid is difficult. It is rewarding because you get to spend time with them but there are many obstacles. Other players and parents are quick to make accusations of favoritism. At the end of a rough practice, match or game you have to take the player home, feed them, and be their parent. There can be baggage brought home from a practice. Many pitfalls can be met. John and I are fortunate to coach our daughters in individual sports with little subjectivity. In golf, the low score wins. I was far harder on my daughter than other players. I held her to a higher standard than other players and I was far less tolerant of poor practice habits than I was with other players. However, I was able to help her in ways I couldn't help other players.

Lainey and I had spent so much time together that a bunch of words were often unnecessary. I knew what motivated her and I knew what buttons to press to get her fired up. Lainey grew up going to basketball practices with me and going to golf events with me. She knew my expectations of players and coaches. She witnessed how I talk to players and she knew my coaching style inside and out. This helped her become a translator. The most important factor for Lainey becoming a master translator was that she cared. If a player doesn't care about performance and improving, then they won't pay attention to the surroundings and communication. A true difficulty in becoming a great athlete is quickly becoming a master translator.

Most players and coaches spend only a few years together, if that. Both coaches and players have languages and it is important for both to learn each other's language. As a player, I have had coaches that I thought were just angry jackwagons who hated me. It turns out they didn't. I had coaches that I thought were good guys and would have my back. It turns out they didn't. I wasn't a very good translator. I only heard their words and I didn't think about what the coach was trying to accomplish with the words. So, I practiced learning how to translate. The first thing I had to do was not let my own thoughts mess up the translation. Many top players are very hard on themselves and use punishing internal dialogue. When a coach approaches a player who is struggling and has some harsh comments, the player's internal dialogue can confuse the translation.

As a coach, to combat the internal dialogue I typically make a joke first. Just a simple light-hearted statement to disrupt the player's internal dialogue is crucial. The next thing I do is find the appropriate level of motivation. Jay's dad knew what Jay was thinking about in that match against RC Speck, so he used it as motivation. John very easily could have said to Jay to "stop worrying about the state tournament lineup, this match has nothing to do with it." But this would not motivate Jay. What John really did was turn Jay's internal dialogue into fire. The soft touch approach is needed with some players and this is the translation breakdown between players and coaches. Coaches have to develop tools to help handle the different communication abilities of players.

An important tool for coaches is not to take things personally. If I took their behaviors personally, then the translation gets muddled. Earlier I discussed a situation with a recent player, Sarah. She translated a situation terribly wrong and it was costly. On that same team I had another player named Trisha who was the exact opposite of Sarah. Trisha was outspoken and had to have all the latest technology and attire and often told people how good she was. She also had a dozen coaches, none of which were me. Early in her golf career I approached her during a tournament. I noticed that she was using the wrong club so I told her to use an 8-iron. Now, all I said is that the pitching wedge in her hand was not enough of a club. So, I pulled out the 8-iron and handed it to her. She made a poor swing and rolled the ball. The next day her father shows up before practice to lecture me about coaching his daughter. In his mind, I needed to write a dissertation and present it to Trisha every time I wanted her to do something differently than she was doing. Coaches don't always have time to do things like that during competition. Coaches are relying on the respect of the players to trust them. During practice is when things can be explained in detail to provide understanding for the future. It is certainly annoying to have a player who doesn't respect the coach or trust the coach, but coaches can't take it personally. Players can't take it personally either. Jay knew that his dad had only Jay's best interest in mind when he fired him up. Jay's younger sister, Nickie, a great player herself, often took things too personally. John coached Nickie in a similar way to Jay but the results were different. While Jay would sort of absorb it, Nickie was a bit readier to fire back, and that did not always end so well. John would remove her from the practice and off to the car she would go. Nickie spent a lot of her summer practice time in the car. Instead of turning the coach's words into fire, she let it make her so angry she couldn't perform.

Jays turn: My sister, Nickie, and I are about as close as a brother and sister can be, and this to some can be a bit surprising, because we are very different people. Mike is right. Nickie reacted much differently to my dad's coaching than I did. I sometimes wonder if it was because she, at a young age, watched her brother get yelled at so much, that she may have been like "If I am ever in that situation, I am NOT putting up with that!" This IS the same person who at five years old, refused to play tennis with her actual dominant hand (left) because at that time, our dad (a righty) was able to beat me (a lefty). Whatever the reason, I believe that even Nickie would agree now that her "stubbornness" held back some of her development. However, she DID end her college career as the Scholar-Athlete of the Year at the University of Cincinnati, so apparently she did "just fine!" For me though, the translating came from a survival mode, but the motivation to learn to do it came from my trust that my dad (as Mike mentioned) always had MY best interest in mind. He was essentially my Mr. Miyagi. I abided by the agreement: "I train, you listen. I say. You do. Now paint the fence."

There was a day when I was 14 years old, that my dad drove me home after a tough practice. It was one of many days that I would end up crying during or after practice, and on this day,

I cried most of the way home. As we pulled into the garage, my dad took a breath, and then asked me an important question that I'll never forget. He said: "Jay, some people at the club have been saying that I am too tough on you. If you agree, and you would like me to lighten up, I will do that." Now, a HUGE part of me wanted to say: "Well of course you are too tough on me!!!!" But the other side of me felt two things. First, how soft would my dad think I was if I agreed to this?! And second, I knew deep down that all of the tough love WAS actually that. It was love. He loved me so much that he just wanted me to do everything I could to reach my potential. Did he go a little overboard at times? Probably yes. But no coach is perfect, right? I know that I am not!

Interestingly, a few years ago, in the middle of a family dinner, my dad sort of began an announcement of sorts. He started to talk about how tough he was on me and tried to apologize. I stopped him before the apology could start. I told him this: "Dad, we all know why you were tough on me. You are competitive and you saw that in me as well, and you needed to do everything you could to help me develop that. I get it. But also, all of the tough times I faced only made me stronger and tougher as a person, and that carried over not just on the tennis court, but into my life. I went through a devastating blow at Bowling Green when my team was cut. I went through a tough divorce. I went through some betrayal at Brown. I would not have been able to handle any of those things and remained sane, let alone continued to be pretty darn successful in my next business endeavors, had it not been for the type of training I was faced with having my dad as my coach. So Dad, once again, no apologies needed. Just a thank you from me to be accepted please."

Mike returns: There is a lot to unpack in what Jay just wrote. An interesting social experiment would be to study the responses from various readers. What is the coach's takeaway? What is the parent's takeaway? And of course, what is the player's takeaway? I was at some of the practices in which Jay thought his dad (coach) was being too tough on him. As a player watching him run some line drills until he cried, I often was glad it wasn't me. However, there were times that I was envious of Jay. I wanted the coach to take an interest in me and push me like that. I believe most players believe they can be the best performers, but each player needs a coach to pull out the potential into performance. I was just the player on that team that got thrown into the shower with his clothes after most practices. Was Jay's dad taking "turning potential into performance" too far? No way!

As a coach I see what John did with Jay another way. Not only was John helping Jay become a performer, he was setting an example for the rest of the team. Now, Jay probably thought at the time that he wasn't doing anything wrong and John was just picking on him. That was actually not the case. John never once just randomly made Jay run a set of lines. Jay could be a bit of a smartass; he could get distracted, and he could also not give the right effort. No coach should let players do any of those things. John was holding Jay accountable. Over the last couple of years, John has turned to me for a little help with his golf swing. I have found that just as John was tough on Jay when he wasn't performing, John is equally tough on himself for underperforming. John is currently 75 years old with a replaced knee and a bum hip. John still expects to swing like he is 35. I subtly try to tell John that he needs to be good with his current swing (it is actually very good for someone with lower body issues). Being technically sound at 75 is rare but John pushes himself to be that rare person. As a coach it is both difficult and admirable to watch.

As a parent I think how John coached Jay is awesome. I know many parents today would disagree. Do parents want coaches to just say how wonderful their child is or do the parents want their child to actually be a good performer? Parents can't have it both ways! To build a performer, coaches have to push their athletes, and that means holding them accountable when they aren't doing all they can to help themselves. John may have treated Jay differently than other players and really came down hard on him when he was underperforming, but he also let everyone know when Jay performed well. He blended the criticism with compliments.

> **Jay brings it home:** Wow, this chapter is bringing back some distinct and powerful feelings! Reading Mike's views of admiration takes me back to watching how my dad pushed countless high school basketball players. I used to sneak into the locker room just before halftime of games and hide in the showers just to be able to listen to my dad's speeches and rants. They were often epic, and I think maybe I was a bit envious of those kids getting yelled at too! That may sound strange to some reading this, but realize that I also got to go watch the second half of those games and witnessed the incredible performance enhancement that almost always took place. It was as if my dad's tirades were **verbal steroids**. Thanks again, Dad! And yes, thank you, Mom! I also realize I wouldn't have survived any of this without you!!

MIDWEST MEETS THE EAST COAST
THINKER V. REACTOR

> *Be Americans. Let there be no sectionalism, no North, South, East or West. You are all dependent on one another and should be one in union. In one word, be a nation. Be Americans, and be true to yourself.*
>
> —George Washington

Jay was once the Head Men's Tennis Coach at Bowling Green State University in Ohio. He then moved on to Brown University. These are two very different universities. Not better or worse, just different. After Jay got settled in Providence, Rhode Island, he invited me to the east coast. I had been east several times before, including a trip to Rhode Island. I have to admit I don't remember my first trip to Rhode Island when I was in middle school but I remember my first trip to see Jay at Brown University. The night before I was supposed to leave Ohio, Jay gave me a call. I only remember one thing from the conversation. He told me not to wear my flannels. Apparently, wearing warm and comfortable clothes in the winter time is a Midwestern fashion. Jay said no one wears flannel in Rhode Island. Why in the Hell not? We argued for hours about this. I understand that Jay just wanted me to feel comfortable and fit into the environment. But that just wouldn't do. Of course, I walked off the plane wearing my flannel shirt. It was the only type of shirt I brought on the trip.

On the way to his house we decided to stop and have some tea (it wasn't tea). We walk into the bar and I kid you not, every guy is wearing black denim pants, a black shirt, and their hair is all gelled up and slicked back. It was exactly as Jay described on the phone.

The next night we went for some tea at a different bar and it was the same thing. What is up with Rhode Island? Why did every guy look like they walked off the set of a Martin Scorsese film? Those men in those bars were being who they were, just as I was being who I am. I am from Ohio, the Midwest, and that is who I always will be.

When I was in college I took a trip with my roommate, Curtis, to Manhattan. My mother arranged an opportunity for us to follow a trader around the floor of the New York Stock Exchange. We were going to FAO Schwartz and all the other tourist activities. While we were there we wanted to meet a former classmate, Braden, who was working there. We found the building Braden was working at with much difficulty. Apparently, there are many buildings in NYC with the name Morgan on it. I guess J.P. Morgan was a big deal. Curtis and I made our way up to the right floor and approached the front desk where two women were working. As we got to the counter of the desk the women were working at, one of the women looked up at us with a face that wasn't enjoying her day. Curtis, with typical Ohio manners, asked if we could please see Braden Kelly. I interjected with a smile, "I hope we have the right floor." The woman asked us if he was expecting us, and we said no, but we understand if he is busy. The second woman at the desk leaned in and asked us, "You guys are from Ohio, aren't you?" How did she know? We said yes, and she said, "Of course you are, you're polite."

Midwesterners have their impressions of the east coast and the east coast cats have their impressions of Midwesterners. I don't know how accurate the stereotypes are, but there is definitely a difference in the lifestyle. I was in Boston in the early 1990s. I was driving my Ford Festiva, which was an amazing engineering accomplishment. I was stopped at a traffic light and I was the first car in the long line waiting for the light to turn green. Just before the light turned green a few cars stopped behind me started to honk their horns. In Boston, you have to anticipate when the light will turn green and already be accelerating through the intersection. It is a fast-paced lifestyle. I don't know why a New England resident would vacation in Florida.

MIDWEST MEETS THE EAST COAST

In the South, the pace of play is slow. It fits my lifestyle but New Englanders have to go insane there.

> **Jay chimes in:** I had lived in Rhode Island for about a year, and on a certain beautiful spring day, I was driving to work. Just before jumping on the highway, I was waiting at the light. Now, having lived in the east for a year, I was well aware that I needed to be ready to go with the light turned green, and because of that, I was incredibly focused and ready to hit the gas pedal. Just before the light turned green, yes BEFORE, the car behind me gave me a little honk. I heard the honk, then saw the light turn green, and instead of going, I paused. I was like "Now wait a darn minute! It hadn't even turned green yet!" So, instead of accelerating through the intersection, I threw my car into park, got out of my car, and casually walked back to the car behind me. As I approached the honker, I could tell that she was getting more and more anxious as I took each step closer. When I got to within 10 feet of the car, I gave her the universal rolling of the window down gesture (kids now won't even know what I'm talking about! Ha). The honker lowered her window about halfway and gave me a look saying "What do you want?!" I then took another step closer and simply said: "I really hope you have a great day today," and then I returned to my car and drove to work. The Midwest meets the East Coast right there!

Back to Mike: When it comes to athletics there is a difference as well. According to Jay, Midwesterners are thinkers. I'm not sure how that correlates though. East coast student-athletes are very concerned about being an Ivy Leaguer. Not too many student-athletes from the Midwest have that on their radar. Ohio is a state known for producing great athletes. I want to list some of them.

1. LeBron James (NBA)
2. Jack Nicklaus (PGA)
3. Simon Biles (U.S. Gymnastics)
4. Ken Griffey, Jr. (MLB)
5. Jerry Lucas (NBA)
6. John Havlicek (NBA)
7. Steph Curry (NBA)
8. Katie Smith (WNBA)
9. Blaine Wilson (U.S. Gymnastics)
10. Roger Clemens (MLB)
11. Mike Schmidt (MLB)
12. Edwin Moses (U.S. Track and Field)
13. Cy Young (MLB)
14. Archie Griffin (NCAA and NFL)
15. Hugh Douglas (Boxing)

These, I hope, are very recognizable names. They are Hall of Famers, and there are many more names I could add to the list. There are some other states that have had the same impact on sports. Texas, Florida, California, and Illinois are hotspots for college recruiters. What makes Ohio such an important state for athletics? Is it the heritage of who settled Ohio? Is it the Midwestern work ethic? Is it an opportunity that Ohioans have over athletes from the east coast? Or, is it all of the above?

I read a book by Malcolm Gladwell, called *Outliers*. In the book, Gladwell tries to account for excellence. One of the things he postulated was that Bill Gates was only Bill Gates because he had access to a computer in 1971, when he was 18 years old. He also postulated that you should never call a person from Kentucky an "A-hole." The Scottish heritage of those who settled in Kentucky believe this is the worst thing to be called. Immigrants from Scotland settled into Kentucky for a couple of reasons. One reason is that most of the good land on the east coast was taken from immigrants from England. Another reason is that the terrain of Kentucky is similar to Scotland and they could raise sheep. The Midwest was settled mostly by German immigrants. There is considerable evidence of the German settlement of the old northwest by the names of the towns. Immigrants in the Midwest had to build everything. They had to clear the trees, till the soil, plant their crops, cultivate the land, build their homes, build their churches and build their towns. There was a tremendous amount of work ethic behind the success of the Midwest. This work ethic was passed down to future generations.

The Midwest also has the space available for athletic success. Tennis courts are not built on top of buildings like they are on the East Coast. Parks are plentiful, baseball fields are plentiful, basketball courts are plentiful, and opportunities to play multiple sports are plentiful. In addition to playing opportunities being plentiful there is safety in the Midwest. Parents are comfortable allowing their children to go out unsupervised and just play. Parents don't do this enough, but the safety is there.

Ohioans have more opportunities to play multiple sports. They have the space and the population. At an early age, kids can play baseball, softball, soccer, golf, tennis, ice hockey, and basketball. By the time they get to middle school, football, wrestling, and lacrosse are available. These sports are offered through public school so the cost is low. Being able to play so many sports at competitive levels makes young athletes more and more competitive. To get an advantage, athletes develop the mental side of athletics.

Unorganized competition allows for greater growth. One of the fundamental principles of athletics that led me into a career in coaching was what athletics can teach young people. As Jay and I work on this project, we constantly discuss the benefits of athletics. Unstructured play or competition allows a young person to develop skills that will make them successful. Ohio has the motto "The Heart of it All." I believe this includes success. Ohio has produced the following successful people in a variety of areas.

Billionaires/Tycoons

1. The Lerner Family
2. Alex Troendle
3. Clayton Mathile
4. Denise York and Family
5. Les Wexner
6. John Rockefeller

Authors

1. Gloria Steinheim
2. Toni Morrison

Astronauts

1. Neil Armstrong
2. John Glenn

Presidents

3. U.S. Grant *(sorry, Illinois, but he was born in Ohio)*
4. William Taft
5. James Garfield
6. Rutherford Hayes
7. Benjamin Harrison
8. William McKinley
9. Warren Harding

Inventors

1. The Wright Brothers
2. Thomas Edison

Entertainers

1. Roy Rogers
2. Dean Martin
3. Dwight Yoakam
4. Machine Gun Kelly
5. Paul Newman
6. Clark Gable
7. Burgess Meredith
8. Bow Wow
9. Arsenio Hall
10. John Legend

Jay is back: Mike, don't forget about Steven Spielberg, Halle Berry, Katie Holmes (she actually dated an Ohio player of mine!), Dave Chappelle and of course Carmen Electra! And I realize that Pete Rose may not be able to get inducted into the MLB Hall of Fame, but we can surely mention Charlie Hustle here!

As Mike mentioned, having grown up in Ohio and now living in New York myself, I tend to feel that Ohioans are more likely to think first, before reacting, and many New Yorkers have no issue with the quick reaction before really thinking things through. At my tennis club in New York, I'm known as a Jedi problem solver. When a tough member presents themselves to my staff, I am often brought in to help. I've been yelled at a lot by these tough members, and my method is to listen patiently, wait them out a bit, and when there is an opening to steer the conversation in a direction I would like, I slide in and shift things to the point that after a couple of minutes, a listener would think that I was giving an educational lecture. I've literally been asked by members that are yelling at me: "Why are you not yelling back?" My typical answer is: "I am just listening to your perspective. It's a little off, but that's ok. I'll keep listening, and then I'll help you." Here is an exact response I once had to a particularly rude member:

"I recognize that everyone has different sensibilities. I do. However, questioning the general manager of a club as to why they even have a front desk attendant, or saying that they are not doing their job when you literally have no idea what the real story was, just because you were frustrated that some extremely cute four-year olds were having the time of their young lives on a court that is about 100 feet from where you are playing is just NOT a response that I am going to have respect for. Not realizing that a better approach would have been to ask what happened, or even say thank you when I emailed you essentially immediately after receiving your email with a solution is just something that I am disappointed in. If you think that your email to me was appropriate and you are fine treating and talking about others like that, then I guess we just have very different values. So, instead of assuming our front desk attendant is worthless, maybe keep in mind that sometimes, just sometimes, you may not know the full story. Maybe you can show a bit more empathy towards others instead of judging them so harshly. Or maybe those are only my Midwestern beliefs and I should just keep them to myself, or maybe just share them with those I am sure will value them. I am not sure if you value them. Maybe you can read all this and it helps you realize something, or maybe not. I guess it's your choice. Believe it or not, this conversation almost immediately turned into a positive back and forth. This member not only apologized, but also began asking questions about my Midwestern values. She later wrote me this: "Oh boy ... There are big differences. DO keep these great emails coming my way. Since your first long email on Tuesday, I actually began the book, "Mindset." A few years ago I would have considered it to be too lame. Now it's a positive influence. THANK you. I might not finish the book, but the fact I started on it, is a good sign."

The moral of the story is that everyone is moldable, even those in the East!

Mike thinks, then reacts: I am not sure what I am reacting to here. I would like to think that everyone is moldable. However, history has proven otherwise, but that doesn't mean I won't keep trying. I get excited every time I get to go to the East Coast to see Jay. Then after an hour of being there I can't wait to get home. I grew up with a lot of space around me and that is what I prefer. New Yorkers are great because they love the way they live, and I respect it. I just don't want it for myself. I was recently in a seminar with people from all over the nation. I was sitting next to a woman from California, and during a break we began talking about the Amish. In this part of Ohio, there are many Amish communities. This lady wanted to go to some Amish stores and have that quaint experience. As we were talking she asked me about something she saw on her drive into town. She noticed some open wood huts by the side of the road that had produce in them. I told her that those were produce stands that Amish use to sell their crops. The woman said, "Yeah, but there wasn't anyone there selling the produce." I then explained that they run on the honor system. The Amish can't spend all day standing by the side of the road; they have chores to do on their farms. They leave the produce there with a list of prices and the customer just puts the money in the box and takes what they need. Now, I am not exaggerating when I tell you that the woman stared at me in silence for several seconds contemplating what I just told her. The idea of the honor system was so alien that she couldn't process it. Don't be fooled; sometimes people do steal in the Midwest, but the system works, and it's cool to be near.

> **Jay concludes:** There are of course many great people in the East as well and I have been lucky enough to be around some of the greatest including my times with John McEnroe and Sean Hannity, my former player and current business partner Mike Kossoff and of course my better half, Sharon Rappaport! Different isn't always bad. It's just different. Sharon and I were recently deciding where to go out to eat in my Ohio hometown when someone suggested to her that we should try the newish Filipino restaurant "downtown." Sharon was super excited to try, but when friends and family shared with us that they had heard the place was bad and about to close, we both hesitated. However, we are both

anything but followers, so we went on our own to check out Deja Food in Mansfield, Ohio. And guess what?! It was super good, even though there were only a handful of customers partaking. Sharon was a bit bummed about the seemingly lack of community support for this hidden gem, and she theorized that maybe the Midwesterners are a bit used to their comfort zone, and maybe, just maybe, they are a bit hesitant to climb into the unknown. I get that feeling at times when I talk to some of my Ohio friends who view New York as a faraway place that would be "crazy to visit one day." And of course Mike will often ask: "Do those people know they don't have to live like that?" Sharon would ask: "why can't they just try it?" I'll be honest here. I absolutely love that I've been able to have had the best of both worlds. I was brought up in the Midwest with values I hold onto deeply, and I get to experience the fast-paced life and extreme diversity of people and personality types here on the East Coast, both in Rhode Island and New York. And I believe it's not at all a coincidence that my best friend is a guy I met in an Ohio grade school, and that my fiancée is a Filipino-Italian woman who grew up on Long Island. This all sounds like a pretty perfect set-up to me!!

Mike's Final Thought: Know thyself. Take full advantage of the surroundings, and if need be, create your surroundings. Find places to play. I used to play basketball in my family room with a pair of rolled up socks and a laundry basket. Know if you are a thinker or a reactor, and embrace it.

APPROACHING THE CHEATERS

If you have integrity, nothing else matters. If you don't have integrity, nothing else matters.

—Alan K Simpson

Courage is being scared to death, but saddling up anyway.

—John Wayne

In the summer of 1983, I was playing in my first ever tennis tournament. I had been taking lessons for a few months, so this was a great first test at the Miss Ohio tournament. After signing me up, my dad told me that the winner and runner-up for each division received a trophy and a kiss from Miss Ohio. All I could think of was that I, at the age of 11, could have the great pleasure to not only receive a trophy from Miss Ohio herself, but also to get a kiss! Needless to say, I was pretty excited about this tournament!

After taking out the number three seed in the first round and then beating my friend, Brett Kaufman, in the quarters, I was set to face number two seed, Jason Voelp, in the semis. To be honest, I didn't think too much about what my opponent's skill level was; I was solely focused on figuring out how to win so I could have a date with destiny, a kiss from Miss Ohio. My eye was on the prize. In the first set I battled harder than I had ever battled for anything in my entire life up to that point, and I took the set 7-5. Then in the second, I went up 5-3, and I started to see visions of Miss Ohio handing me the trophy and giving me that kiss. However, Jason had other designs. He made a comeback winning the next game at love, and then going up 40-15 for the chance to tie the set at 5-5. I then dug deep thinking about Miss Ohio, and won the next four points to take the match 7-5, 6-4. Now, it is customary at the end of a tennis match to go and shake the hand of your opponent. I was a new tournament player of course, but I had already learned this protocol. So, as excited as I was having just earned the spot on the podium with Miss Ohio, I knew I had to go to shake Jason's hand. I walked up to the net, but Jason stayed back at the baseline. I was greatly confused because I knew Jason played many tournaments, and thus, he, of course, would understand the need for the customary post-match handshake. As I approached the net, he was looking at me and finally asked me, "What are you doing?" I quickly responded, "Coming up to shake your hand!". He then replied, "It's 5-5." Now, he and I both knew that I had won the match. However, Jason took the opportunity with no referee present to change the score, preventing the ending for his own hopes of meeting this Miss Ohio. I was beside myself! How could someone just change the score like that? The match is over! I had won! I was going to kiss Miss Ohio! And now this asshole is changing the score? After the match is over he does this? The tournament Director, Ron Schaub (who later became my longtime coach alongside my dad), walked out to the court to address the two arguing boys. Using proper tennis rules, because we could not agree on the score, we had to go back to the last agreeable score, and so we were forced to resume the second set with the score tied at 3-3. I was so upset I could barely make contact with the ball for the next two games, and went down 3-5. Then, I saw an image. It was kind of like when Princess Leia knelt down to slide the stolen Death Star plans into R2-D2's cartridge holder, and made a plea to Obi-Wan, saying that he was their only hope. For me, my image was Miss Ohio! I looked across the net at Jason, and then decided that this bully was going down. I won the next four games, taking that match again with the final score being 7-5, 7-5. I did lose in the finals to Doug Hartzler (a loss I would avenge for my first News Journal title a month later), but I captured my prize, a date with Miss Ohio the next weekend. So, at the end of the Miss Ohio parade in the metropolis of Mansfield, Ohio, I got to go on stage, and receive a trophy from THE Miss Ohio. Now to be completely honest, I'm not sure if Miss Ohio gave me a kiss or not because I totally blacked out walking up on that stage, but when I walked off and asked my dad if she gave me a kiss, he assured me that she did.

Unfortunately, junior tennis is riddled with stories like this. Most tournaments and matches are played with very little officiating. Tennis is still sort of known as this old school sport, a gentleman's sport you could say, where players are supposed to have honor and not cheat. The common rule of thumb we were all taught as kids was if you weren't sure if a ball was in or out, you were supposed to give the benefit of the doubt to your opponent and call it in. However, the more common cliché used was: "When in doubt, call it out!" I've had countless bad calls made against me, and I've made some bad calls myself for sure. I definitely didn't always handle getting cheated (otherwise known as hooking) on the tennis court well, but as I became a better and better competitor, I developed some very distinct methods for handling it.

Mike adds: Wow, someone cheating at tennis? That doesn't seem right. Next thing I know; people will be cheating at golf! I joke to mask the anger. Cheating at sports is an absolute sin. It happens in many sports far too often. The big question that each cheater needs to ask themselves is, "What did I gain?" The truth about cheating is this: once a cheater, always a cheater. At the beginning of each golf season I always start with the above statement.

Cheating in sports is pervasive. There was spygate in the NFL, stealing signs in MLB, doping by the Russian Olympic Team (multiple sports), doping in MMA, Lance Armstrong doping, and the list can go on and on. I believe the most widespread cheating happens on the golf course or tennis court, specifically among amateur athletes. It is very easy to move the golf ball to a better spot, or to drop a ball in play when you know a ball is OB, or simply lie about the score on a hole. In tennis the cheating is more about the lines than the score. Although, I did have a similar experience as Jay when trying to qualify for the tournament team playing tennis my freshman year at Lexington High School. Earlier, I discussed having to qualify for the sectional tournament and my opponent had issues with the correct score. That is when I learned to not just call the score after every point, but to be sure my opponent agrees.

When I have my parent/player meeting at the beginning of each golf season I always discuss "once a cheater, always a cheater." I tell the players and parents about an incident that occurred at the sectional tournament when a freshman player for another school went 15 strokes below her average to win the tournament. The player was put into a twosome instead of the typical threesome and her playing partner was new to the game. The player 100% did not beat her average by 15. In fact, I didn't see her hit one good shot. Four years later, when this player was wrapping up her high school golf career, she was still labeled a cheater. It was still widely discussed around the district. That particular player may have never cheated again. She was young and made a mistake, but that mistake would be carried with her for a very long time. So, I ask my players, "Is it worth it? Are a few strokes worth your integrity and reputation?"

I tell the "once a cheater, always a cheater" story for two reasons: first, to make my team think about their reputation or legacy and second, to let them know what their responsibilities are as a member of the team and as a golfer. Like tennis, players have to police themselves. Golf is a game of honor and integrity. A golfer must protect the game and the field. Players on other parts of the golf course are dependent on each player enforcing the rules and ensuring that no one is cheating. I understand how uncomfortable it is to question the integrity of another person. A player never knows how the cheater is going to respond, but it is a responsibility to approach a cheater. A player may accuse you of cheating; they may get angry and start yelling; or they may use social media to bully you. I guess there are many different scenarios, but the uncomfortable things have to be done.

I always advise my players to never give an opponent the opportunity to cheat. For example, don't ask a player what their score was on a hole. Tell them what their score was on a hole. Always help a player look for their ball so they can't locate the wrong ball or illegally drop a ball into play. Be a part of the opponent's game and not a spectator. However, if you do believe an opponent has cheated, then you must confront the situation with a smile. Start the conversation with the words, "Are you sure you had a five, because I thought it was a six?" There is no accusation in that sentence, it is a question. If the opponent is adamant that they had a five, then the two players should count out the entire hole. If the two still disagree (they won't), get a coach or official. I understand that many negative actions could occur at this point, but it is a requirement and must be done. In addition, the one positive outweighs the negatives. The positive is that you have your integrity. As a coach, this is one of the things that you hope athletics teaches a young person.

On Sunday nights at the high school there is a pick-up basketball game for adults. The game is open to anyone out of high school in the area. Typically, 15 to 20 guys show up. A few guys pick teams and it is a five on five game. Most of the players are just there to get some exercise. However, some are there to relive their glory days and take things a little too serious. One guy who played most weeks is Mark. Now Mark used to play fullback for the University of Arkansas. He is 6'1" and 260 pounds, and he lived in the gym. Mark was always arguing about the score and every time he missed a shot he claimed he was fouled. Sometimes when he would argue about the score he was right and other times he was wrong. This particular Sunday night Mark was wrong. I wasn't in the game but I was sitting off to the side watching. For several trips down the floor he was calling out the wrong score and the other team would just accept it. Most likely, because they were afraid of Mark. After another questionable foul call by Mark he called out the score of 9-8, his team was up. I immediately yelled "BS" onto the court. I did a couple of things wrong here. I used a confrontational word instead of posing a question. Next, I said it as I was walking toward Mark. This is confrontational as well. So I created an uncomfortable situation. I don't really recall the next few minutes that clearly because my adrenaline level was skyrocketing. I knew I was in it now. Jay was actually visiting Lexington at the time for the holidays and he had to tell me what happened.

Mark and I were nose to nose arguing about the score. This is a guy that if he landed one punch would really ruin my night and probably the next several nights. I didn't back down though. I went point by point and the score was 9-8 alright, but Mark's team was losing. I guess during the yelling phase of the conversation I even told him to stop being soft and that he called too many fouls. I used way more colorful language than that. Mark also called me a few things, but thankfully no punches were thrown. During the entire exchange I was scared and uncomfortable, but when it was over I felt great. Several other players discreetly thanked me. They did this discreetly because we don't want to show up another player. The next week, Mark showed up again. I thought he might take a week or two off but he didn't. In fact, when he walked into the gym he came over and sat next to me and we politely talked about nothing in particular. The confrontation ended with the best case scenario. No one was punched and Mark toned down his basketball rage.

Jay, what should a player do when they are being cheated, or when they witness cheating?

> **Jay answers with no rage:** Well Mike, I like the acknowledgement of the importance of being less accusatory and refraining from direct confrontation. This is equally important on the tennis court. When a tennis player gets hooked (cheated), one of three things happen.

1. The player doesn't notice or doesn't seem to notice, which allows the cheater to feel comfortable with cheating later in the match.

2. The player gets super upset about the cheating, which almost motivates the cheater to cheat more, because anyone knows that it is much easier to beat someone who is super emotional.

3. The cheater is "approached" calmly and casually.

Approaching a cheater goes a bit like this for me and this is what I teach my players: When my opponent cheats me, I first get a bit excited. I know this is a strange reaction, but one has to admit, this is a much better emotion than to be angry about being cheated. After quickly calming my initial excitement, I walk super slowly to the net, glaring over to the spot where the ball bounced with no words said. This often freaks my opponent out a bit, or at least annoys them greatly. I look calmly at the line my ball hit, and then casually back at my opponent, then back to the line, and I repeat this until I feel I have crawled a little into the brain of my opponent. Now, usually it doesn't go past that. However, sometimes, a cheater is a true cheater and will do it again. At that point, I again walk to the net and subtle things are said like: "Oh, so you are going to call that out, heh? I guess I'll have to call lines out too." Or I might say: "Hey, I just want to make sure that you are taking that point. We both know I won it, but if you need the point, I guess that's okay." Without having to dive to my cheating opponent's level and actually cheat him back, my subtle or at times not so subtle threat forces my opponent to play much more conservatively, avoiding the boundaries of the court in fear that they may be cheated. To me, it is a genius way to make a cheater play to a lower level, and this of course makes them easier to beat, which is what they deserve ... to be beaten!

At 54 years old, my old man's doubles partner, Will Calhoun, and I are #1 in the country (another fun update to share!). In a recent tournament semifinal match where I was actually playing with a substitute partner because Will had to take his daughter to a Taylor Swift concert (true story!), my sub and I were up 7-6, 6-5, 40-15 with our opponents serving to us, one point away from a win. After my partner's mis-hit return landed a couple of inches inside the line and we began to walk to the net somewhat apologetically to shake hands at the end of the match, the server called the ball out. I was like: "Wait, what?" Our opponent claimed out loud that it was a foot out. I laughed a bit (couldn't help it) and walked up to the net to look where the ball landed. I said: "The ball was 2 inches INSIDE the line, but if you want to call that out, I guess it's your call." I then walked back to the baseline to prepare for the serve to come to me, still with a matchpoint. As I turned around, the server pointed at the ground, tapping his racquet on a spot a foot behind the baseline. Big mistake. Big. I then walked super slowly up to the net, and simply said: "Look, the ball was two inches in. If you claim it was two inches out, then I'll give you a pass. But do NOT say it was a foot out again. That just makes you look ridiculous." I went back to the baseline. The cheater then missed both serves badly, double faulting and giving the match to us. Whoever penned "cheaters never win" loved that ending for sure.

Mike calmly responds: I am not sure why I have to calmly respond. There is a part of me that wants to respond in all CAPS! I don't know if I have ever watched Jay play a tennis match without a similar interaction as he mentions above. Sometimes it can be very hard to watch. I often have to walk away. Golf is a much different sport. In tennis, as well as many sports, you are playing against a person who wants to win just as badly as you want to win. In golf (unless it is matchplay) there are two opponents. The golf course and yourself. The golf course doesn't care if it wins or loses. As long as the course gets a little water, a little sun, and a little fertilizer, it wins. The course doesn't care if you shoot a 70 or 110. A golfer's own mind can unfortunately be the toughest opponent. But that is for a different chapter. In a golf tournament there are human opponents. What is difficult about a golf tournament is that you have no control over your opponents. In fact, you only see two or three of them. There are 100 opponents scattered over 150 acres, and you have no idea what they are doing.

It is the golfer's responsibility to protect the field. A golfer has to ensure the integrity of all players in their group. This means you have to approach the cheaters. Not long ago, my team was involved in a tournament and a player on another team was having trouble keeping track of their score. My player and another player in the group brought this to my attention. So, I called that particular player's coach. I told him that there are some scoring discrepancies and he needs to check it out. Unfortunately, he didn't. A few holes later the problem was persisting. I again told the coach to get involved. He did not. I watched the group play a hole and sure enough the player did not record an accurate score. So, I called a different coach to come watch. The same thing happened. This was definitely a problem. My player was getting frustrated and losing focus on her own game. She and the other players in the group were spending so much energy trying to keep an honest score. I told the players to continue to write the score down that the player in question said, and write down the score they believed she had. I didn't want my player to not be a performer because she was concentrating on policing. Unfortunately, the issue was never resolved and the cheater was able to keep her score and her team won the tournament.

Jay finishes off the cheaters: Mike is right, sometimes the cheaters do win, at least in that particular moment. But I think we both have the same ideals in that we believe that in the end, when certain final judgments are made, those cheaters will not end up in the winner's circle. Now, I am not sure if this "final judgment" needs to happen by the end of a match or game, or if it catches up to the cheaters at the end of a season or year, or if the judgment only is made at the end-end. Whichever it is, I encourage everyone to give the cheaters a chance to correct their actions first, and to do it as calmly as possible. I had to remind a particular opponent this summer that he "is better than that" after a particularly bad cheating attempt, and my hope is that he heard me, and will allow his own character to grow because of that altercation. At the end of the day, I am just out here trying to do my best to make the most positive impacts daily with those people who allow me to do so!

YOU ALWAYS GOT MORE TO GIVE

Strength does not come from physical capacity.
It comes from an indomitable will.

—Mahatma Gandhi

One of my favorite players of all time, Matt Wiles, once sent me a bit of a rant that he had written down. Matt was one of the most competitive players I had ever coached, but also one of the most emotional. We spent a lot of time discussing his ability to control those emotions and develop his skills to do so in order for him to achieve his highest potential as a college tennis player. These experiences are what made this composition that Matt wrote and sent to me while he was in law school so special, and I would like to share it here:

> A wise Falcon, my mentor in BG and now someone's mentor on Wall Street, once told me an adage that he firmly believed in. At the time, the seemingly insignificant, short, grammatically incorrect statement seemed just that – insignificant, short and grammatically incorrect. It was only over this past Christmas break that the truth and power of the piece of wisdom hit me with full force. It is now my motto, and to live by it is to live well. A story will bring it home to you...
>
> A number of weeks before my first finals week in law school, I was studying my butt off in the library. I had been stuffed in this cubicle for the past four hours, going over my notes and flashcards again and again and again. At that moment, I decided to pack it in and go home to watch the much anticipated UC-UNC basketball game. As I was picking up my stuff to leave, I saw a fellow student a couple of cubicles down from me. This kid went to UC (University

of Cincinnati) and had season tickets to their basketball games while enrolled there. He had arrived at the library around the same time as me, but was still buried in his books when I was leaving. I stopped by and asked him if he was going home to watch the game. He picked up his head, briefly stared at me, and replied: "what game?". I told him; he just let out a subtle chuckle, and went back to his books. At the time, I thought nothing of it, and in fact chastised him for being such a dork. Then, near the end of December, about a week after exams were over, it hit me. The wise Falcon's statement flashed in bright lights in my head: "YOU ALWAYS GOT MORE TO GIVE". I next thought back to that night in the library. I realized that, of course, my classmate KNEW of the game. Any dedicated sports fan would, and being fairly close to Cincinnati, it was in all the papers. So, why the "what game" statement? Simple, YOU ALWAYS GOT MORE TO GIVE. Law school, like college tennis, fosters a very competitive environment. All people in law school are fairly smart, all college tennis players are talented. Everyone tries hard, and only in isolated or rare instances will talent alone pull one through; so, what will separate the winners from the losers? The answer is EFFORT. It is that person that is willing to go further than just trying hard that will come out on top. And when you take a test or play a match, and do poorly, it is a cowardly excuse to claim that you 'gave it your best shot'. In the mind of a winner, there is no such thing as a 'best effort'. YOU ALWAYS GOT MORE TO GIVE. Best efforts are something losers claim when what they really mean is quite the opposite. A winner will always find something to improve on, something to work harder at. So, it is not the guy with all the talent and no effort that will prevail. It is the guy who is willing to kill himself until he cannot physically or mentally go anymore, till his body and mind are so exhausted that collapsing is the only thing left to do. It is the guy who, with pride, blood, sweat, and tears, says that he left it ALL out there, and then not gloat in his glory, but immediately find ways to make it even better. It is the guy who is willing to say "what game?" that will ultimately prevail. YOU ALWAYS GOT MORE TO GIVE.

> By the way, the kid who posted the sarcastic question to me, "what game?", is ranked second in our class of 163...

> I always loved this and would read it at least once a month during my college coaching days. It was included in every team handbook that I produced. It is truly inspirational and I am happy to share it here so it can live on and continue to inspire.

Mike adds: Inspiration? I agree with Jay that it is a good anecdote, but what inspires one might not inspire all. Sometimes athletes just aren't listening. They hear so many words from too many people and they become immune to the words. I don't think that I am very smart so if I know something then everyone should know. However, that isn't always the case. Sometimes I hesitate from giving a pep talk because I make the assumption that the players have already heard a similar story. That isn't the case though. More often than not young athletes haven't heard the usual stories in any coach's repertoire. Only 10% of my students have even heard of John Wayne. So, I made the decision to always give the pep talk. If they already heard it, they can hear it again.

Now to Jay's point about always giving more. **No truer words have been written.** I know that from time to time things may look bleak. Sometimes teammates don't perform well. Sometimes the coach is thinking about a fight with their spouse. Sometimes the referees are not calling a good game. Sometimes the spectators are playing on their phones. Sometimes mom or dad make strange faces. A player has to tune all that garbage out. Athletes can't control any of those things. The one constant every player can control is their effort and focus. The human body and mind are the most resilient creations. People can do so much more than they know.

I remember an argument I had with my wife, Audrey. I don't necessarily remember all of the specifics but I remember saying that I was doing the best that I could. This was a lie. Whereas, I was trying hard to be the man that she wanted. I wasn't doing all that I could. I know this to be true because I don't know what my capabilities are.

Just when I think I am doing all that I can, I do more. The thing that hinders athletes the most is the words from too many people. Parents are telling their kids how to play, friends are telling kids how to play, and of course coaches are telling them how to play. It would be great if everyone was saying the same thing to these players but that probably isn't the case. The young athlete is pulled in many directions. To get out of this trap young athletes just stop listening.

The best voice a player listens to is their own voice. The best way for an athlete to listen to their own voice is to create tunnel vision. This is far easier said than done. Sports psychologists have described tunnel vision as being in a flow state or being in the zone. As a coach I have read many books on flow states and I find them fascinating. I prefer referring to this state of mind as tunnel vision. It is easier to create tunnel vision than a flow state. A player can create tunnel vision by focusing on one very specific and small target. In golf a player shouldn't look at the golf ball. A player should look at the 7 o'clock position on a golf ball. A golf ball has a circumference of 5.28 inches. A player should focus on just three dimples of that circumference. By narrowing the focal point, a player's mind is required to focus on a specific task. Since no brain is capable of truly multitasking, the brain is forced to tune out distractions.

> **Jay gives more:** The search for "the zone" is an important undertaking, and in my opinion, a "real competitor" is one who not only strives to make great efforts with all aspects of their abilities to find a state of "the zone," but who also realizes that even when that state was found, and success was the result, there was still **MORE TO GIVE.**

THE ENTITLEMENT MISSION STATEMENT

To understand this rather infamous statement, one must first understand the "Bruno Mantra." At Brown University, I often had to share with my team how they (and other "Ivy Leaguers") were perceived in the outside world. Just one word best described these athletes: SOFT. Thus, one of my goals as an Ivy League coach was to sort of beat the softness out of these Ivy Leaguers, and present a path of goals that pushed us all to become hard-nosed competitors possessing an extreme level of blue-collar work ethic. This was not an easy thing to achieve, but one of my proudest feats as a coach was that I was able to do exactly this, and our teams projected an aura of toughness that was respected and often feared by many of our closest rivals. At one point at Brown University, we considered ourselves so different from the other players of our league that we all often made fun of them calling them the 'incredibly insulting' term, "Ivy Leaguers". No one involved in our program wanted to be called that because it was essentially synonymous with the word: SOFT. Those outside of our program may not have been able to understand that reference, and that was also okay with us.

However, a year after we won our first Ivy League title in 2005, I had a very young team consisting of FIVE first year players (this was literally half of my team!), and even though one of these players was Dan Hanegby, a young man tough enough to have fought for the Israeli Army, we were struggling to live up to the toughness expectations that our past teams had built. So, after a few conversations with a couple of my favorite Bruno guys, Kris Goddard and Ben Brier, they wrote "The Entitlement Mission Statement," and then asked me to share it with the team. We had just had an extremely rough fall season and it seemed like we were on the verge of having a very long and tough year, so the delivery of this "statement" caused some serious fireworks. Now, I'll be honest, when I first shared this with the team, they were not happy at all. In fact, they were very insulted. However, the spirit of this statement sunk in over the course of the season, and...well let me share the statement with you here (I apologize for the "colorful" language), and THEN I will tell you the result:

> *"I played #1 on my high school team"*
> *"I beat Donald Young in the 12s"*
> *"My parents have never said no to me...ever"*
> *"I was ranked top 10 in my section in the juniors"*
> *"I beat Adil in a one-on-one doubles tiebreaker"*
> *"I went 4 and 4 with Drake"*
> *"I've never lost a practice set to Phil"*
> *"I didn't come to Brown to sit on the bench"*
>
> ### I DON'T GIVE A FUCK...YOU'RE NOT ENTITLED TO *SHIT*
>
> *If you win a practice match, you are not entitled to play. If you win a sprint, you are not entitled to play. If you win the "B" flight at the Brown Invy, you are not entitled to play (that is like paring a short par four at Cranston CC and thinking you are ready for the Blue Monster at the Doral). If you beat someone who is currently above you on the team in a baseline game on the varsity courts, you are not entitled to play. If you were a decent junior at best, but suddenly forgot your first week as a freshman that the coach went to bat to get you into an Ivy League school, you are not entitled to play. You gotta go through some things on the Brown tennis team before you gain respect from players and coaches (or walk into the program as a freshman "blue chip" to get that respect, e.g. Justin Natale). Even then, you gotta show your ability to win a big match time and time again (e.g. Adil Shamasdin, Chris Drake) so that the rest of the pussies who think they are entitled can watch and learn. From the famous words of my freshman year*

THE ENTITLEMENT MISSION STATEMENT

"I don't want to see anyone looking around watching to see if other people are winning to let you off the hook. You win your match." It all comes down to this: Being a member of the team and a player in the line-up is a privilege, not a right. Go win a match and you will sleep just fine at night.

FINISH OUT YOUR SPRINTS; DON'T ASK TO LEAVE PRACTICE EARLY; DON'T TELL ME YOU HAVE TO TAKE THAT CLASS WHEN YOU'RE A SOPHOMORE; DON'T TELL ME HOW MUCH BETTER YOU ARE THAN SOMEONE ELSE; DON'T TELL ME YOU ABSOLUTELY HAVE TO GO HOME THIS WEEKEND TO SEE YOUR GIRLFRIEND; TEAM MEETINGS/GATHERINGS ARE NOT SOMETHING YOU TRY TO GET OUT OF; DON'T BITCH ABOUT PLAYING FOOTBALL; TAKE BUTTS-UP LIKE SOMEONE WHO HAS BALLS — NOT SOMEONE WHO'S SCARED OF LOSING THEM; HIT AN EXTRA BUCKET OF SERVES; DON'T GET FUCKED UP 24 HRS BEFORE A MATCH EVEN IF YOU AREN'T IN THE LINEUP; DONT TELL ME COACH IS FUCKING YOU OVER, MAKE IT HAPPEN YOURSELF! PLAYING TENNIS FOR BROWN IS AN ABSOLUTE PRIVILEGE. IT HAS NEVER BEEN A RIGHT; NO MATTER HOW GOOD YOU ARE!

There are so many kids that would die to bleed for Bruno, puke for

Bruno, and sit in the 10-spot just to be a part of Bruno...Never once did I feel entitled to be on the tennis court with my team...I played my whole career with the fear that each year, I was replaceable...Now that I'm a weekend warrior like Briah and so many other Brown tennis alumni, I realize how special it was to be a part of this program... This was my Duke Basketball, my USC Football...Coach will make you realize what you've got even if he has to run you around the fields, chasing you on a bike, or he has to put a football helmet on your head for practice. He'll make you figure it out. He did it last year, and he'll do it again.

This 2006 Bruno Tennis Team not only worked their asses off to strive to meet these toughness expectations, but they actually began to celebrate this Mission Statement, and I believe this was the biggest reason that this team produced one of the most successful seasons in the 100-year history of Brown Tennis! Not only did we win our second Ivy Title in a row (with five new players!), we went on to the NCAA Tournament with incredible performances, almost incredible as the advancement the year before to the Quarterfinals of the NCAA Doubles Tournament by Adil Shamasdin and Phil Charm, giving Brown Tennis their first, and still ONLY All-Americans!

After the 2006 season, senior Luke Tedaldi, a player who had to fight his way just to be ON the team as a freshman and as a senior clinched both the 4-3 win over Harvard to put us in the Ivy League Championship playoff and then the 4-3 win to clinch the Ivy Title and NCAA automatic bid, wrote something that very accurately conveyed the growth that this very special group of athletes experienced in this historic season:

> *It is for those elite few who have braved a sub 5:30 mile, a 7AM pool workout, fast feet until your head aches and your calves burn, and dual matches that are so fierce your soul hurts for days after. You tirelessly pour your blood, sweat and tears into all that is BRUNO, even when the opposition claws at you like a pack of rabid dogs. We remain the best because we work harder than everybody else, sacrificing everything time and time again. Stay strong boys, because when you're on top, teams gun for you with passion that can only come from being beaten down by the Bears!*

Mike reacts: Once I get past the colorful language there is a very valuable takeaway in the mission statement. No one is entitled to anything. A player's performance last week doesn't give them privilege this week. I have had countless players make the assumption that they deserve a certain spot on the team, or minutes in a game because they think they have done something great. What has the player really done? By playing great and doing great, a player simply did what they were supposed to do. When something great is accomplished it should be celebrated at that moment. Then the moment is over. The player needs to get back to work and be better. This is a very simple concept. No one is entitled and no one has privilege. Train and play, train harder and play better, train even harder and play even better.

> **Jay concludes:** As a college coach I was extremely lucky to have coached so many incredible people. I of course have many of my favorites, but what I have always loved is when players experience so much in their time as a member of the program that they want to give back and make sure that their incredible times can be felt by those who come after them. One particular player of mine at Bowling Green, Matt Wiles, wrote something along these lines, but maybe more to give back to his coach:

TO BE A GREAT COACH

To call someone JUST a great coach can be misleading,
For many elements must be satisfied to make the claim.

Sure, a great coach must possess vast
and superior knowledge of the game,
But that alone can, at best,
give one a title of "game expert."

A great coach must also be a great listener,
A person you can explain problems to, a person who lets you vent.

A great coach gives great advice,
Not just about tennis, but about life –

Advice from experience had and lessons learned,
Whether it be a kick in the ass or a hand on the shoulder,
Advice that focuses on you independent from your role as a player.

A great coach is not caught up in the actual wins and losses,
The records and rankings –
The great coach realizes these things reflect only
a small percentage of what you do.

A great coach is more concerned with what you did to get there,
and how you did it.
If you did it with class, hard work and team unity,
The numbers are irrelevant to the great coach.

A great coach sees the practice, matches,
and attitudes from the player's eyes,
And lies awake at night figuring out what went wrong.

THE ENTITLEMENT MISSION STATEMENT

A great coach is passionate about being a coach,
Passionate about the game and results,
But even more passionate about his players,
And determined to improve them athletically and mentally.

A great coach gives his players motivation and confidence,
Willing them to do well, talking them up as the best in the land,

And digging down in the trenches by their sides during conditioning,
To show he believes in them.

Most importantly to me, a great coach is a great friend,
Sometimes wanting to hang out in the hotel room and talk,
Or joining your intramural basketball team to have some fun,
Or playing football on the beach.

A great coach believes in you when no one else does,
When you did not play much your freshman year,
He puts you out there just to show he believes you can do it,
And gives you the opportunity to prove it,
To him, to other teams, to your teammates,
But most importantly to yourself.

A great coach embodies all these roles and more,
And leaders like these will drive players,
To succeed on the court in the form of wins,
Or in the form of added confidence or competitiveness,

To succeed off the court in the classroom,
And give them the discipline and encouragement to go to law school,
And use the lessons learned to be successful there.

I was lucky enough to have a great coach in college,
And am lucky now to count him as my friend.

WHO DO YOU WANT TO BE AS A FUTURE COLLEGE ATHLETE

Too many athletes go to teams that don't welcome them. They aren't understanding the importance of choosing an environment where they can thrive, joining a group that will want them to be successful, and a culture that values each others' individual goals along with the team goals.

— John Harris

I dedicate this chapter to my college teammate and roommate, Kyle Mason, as I write this on a return flight from his funeral. Kyle is gone too early. I miss this amazing guy. I had the opportunity to speak at the service and was able to share some stories and also explain to Kyle's friends and family how Kyle was a guy who no one ever fought with. I fought with other teammates, but never with Kyle. He was the glue to the team and he honestly cared so deeply about all of us. The unique thing about Kyle though was his amazing ability to SHOW us all on the team how much he valued us and wanted us to be successful (and just about everyone else in his life I came to realize yesterday!). If I was going back to college to be an athlete, I would want to be like Kyle!

One of my favorite consultation sessions ever was one where I was working on Danny Pellerito's overall mindset. Early in the session, I asked Danny if he wanted to be a college tennis player and he quickly said yes. I then asked him what he would want college coaches to say about him during the recruiting process. He wasn't so quick to answer this question. I offered some guidance in asking him if he would want a college coach to describe him as tough. He of course said yes. How about reliable? He said yes. I asked, "What else?" Danny then explained how he would like coaches to view him as a great team guy and also a guy who could be put in the toughest of situations and come out with a win. I then shared that I often had heard college coaches referring to the most respected players on certain teams as "tough outs." In the line-up of six singles players, the "tough out" was the toughest spot to win against on that team. I asked Danny if he wanted that to be him. He immediately said YES! I then rehashed that list to Danny, looked at him, and said: "We have a lot of work to do!" This started the "Danny build." We used these very long-term goals to guide us along his junior career. We would often refer back to this list and evaluate if the things Danny was accomplishing and the way he was behaving on the court were in line with these guidelines. Did we need to work harder to make him tougher? Did we need to figure out how to get him to hit bigger in order to develop an aggressive style?

    I now use this method with all of my players who have college tennis aspirations and I believe it is extremely valuable. One of those players was Benji Grossman. Benji essentially came from a family of geniuses, as his oldest brother, Alex, graduated from MIT and his middle brother, Jake, graduated from Amherst and is currently in the University of Michigan Law School. As Benji matriculated through his junior tennis career with aspirations of playing college tennis, he was constantly changing his game. Somewhere along the way, he developed an incredible forehand slice (not necessarily the most common of tennis weapons), and as we worked to build a more standard forehand as his weapon, his results actually worsened even though this more conventional forehand improved greatly. So, during an intense "family meeting," we all decided that we would work to develop "*the style.*" Now, this "*style*" was definitely a bit unorthodox as it was somewhat centered around a slice forehand and a flat backhand as the major weapon, BUT we felt that it fit Benji's grinding mindset, and that combination was what we would be able to sell to college coaches while also realizing that this "style" was what would allow

Benji to be most comfortable, and thus most confident, and then most successful on the court. Fast forward a few years and Benji concluded his college career as his conference tournament MVP where he led MIT to the championship and an NCAA tournament bid. Apparently "the style" was pretty cool!

Mike chimes in: When I was in college we didn't have cable. We just had a television, a VCR, and about three tapes. One of the tapes was *Top Gun*. I have no idea how many times that I have watched that movie but I can quote the heck out of it. I don't simply like the movie because of the great lines in it. I like the relationship between Maverick and Goose. They are the epitome of teamwork. After the release of *Top Gun: Maverick*, many dudes were trying to bring back the mustache. Unfortunately, this trend was hitting high schools. It is rather sad to watch a high school boy try to grow a mustache. I was recently talking to DJ, one of my students trying this fad out. I made a comment about the progress his mustache was making and DJ said to me, "You should grow a mustache." My reply to DJ was very simple. I said, "I'm a Maverick not a Goose." I know what I am and that is a major step in being a successful athlete.

Know your role. This very easily could be the title of the chapter. The first time I watched Top Gun I thought Maverick was just about the coolest character of all time. However, the more I watched the movie the more I saw it wasn't Maverick, the individual; it was Maverick and Goose – the team – that was special. Goose never complained that he was the rear pilot and Maverick was getting the glory. He did his job; he was a great teammate. If there are 12 players on a basketball team, everybody on the team has a role to play. It is the player's duty to play that role to the best of their ability. If the role is to practice hard and be part of the scout team in practice, then be the best scout team player ever. Don't whine and cry about not getting minutes; go help the team win championships. I have been on teams where I was the 12th man and I have been on teams where I was "the guy." I worked hard on both teams.

The team that gave me the most respect was the team where I was the 12th man. During film sessions I paid attention to all the details. It was my job to know the offenses and defenses of the opposing team so during practice I could help my team win. I sat very engaged and my teammates respected me for it. That particular season I turned 16 and it was my only birthday party that I ever had. I was born very close to Christmas and birthdays get overlooked. My teammates were there and they gave me one of the best presents ever. They gave me a Lexington t-shirt and they put the word "coach" on the back of it. The simple gesture made me believe that I was an important part of the team. The team that I was "the guy" on never did anything like that. They just looked at me with disappointment if I had a bad game. People respect hard work and kindness. If a player isn't a good teammate, if they don't work hard all the time, if they are selfish and self-centered, then they become nothing more than cautionary tales. It doesn't matter how much talent a player has; if they are bad teammates, then they will be used by the coach as an example of what not to be at future team meetings.

> **Jay reacts to "the guy"**: Um, you were "the guy" on a team? Was it like a backgammon squad? Haha, just kidding!
> I love the points there, Mike! It actually reminded me of a great speech Bobby Knight once gave about motivation. It goes like this: "You can talk about all of the motivational speeches and phrases and devices in the world, but the greatest motivator of all is your ass on the bench. There is no better motivator. Ass meets bench. Bench retains ass. Ass transmits message to brain. Brain transmits signal to body. Body gets off the bench and plays better." Here is a bit of a secret code for all of the parents out there: ALLOW YOUR KIDS TO LEARN THIS LESSON. If you let the coaches sit your kids on the bench, then you will quite possibly be unlocking the greatest motivational power they've ever had. OR, you can complain to the coach and help your child become

the entitled player college coaches work to avoid in the recruiting process. Who do you want your kids to be?

Mike concludes: Failing is a difficult thing. At least, I hope it doesn't come easy to anyone. People want to be successful in what they do. Failing is a big part of success. I know that seems counterintuitive. I am reminded of Jerry Jones' Hall of Fame induction speech. The Cowboys were playing a preseason game in Japan. The winner of the game received a Samurai Warrior Trophy and the loser of the game received a doll. As the story goes, Jones went over to Head Coach Jimmy Johnson and said he really wanted to win that trophy. That would mean playing the starters the whole game. Johnson didn't want to do that because he wanted his team to be prepared for the season. He wanted them prepared for long-term success, not immediate short-term success. Johnson won the argument and the Cowboys stuck to the original plan. The Cowboys lost the preseason game, but five months later the Cowboys lifted the Lombardi Trophy. So, to add to the notion that Jay mentioned to parents, let the bench be a catapult for a player's success. If the player wants to be successful, they will practice a little harder, try a little harder, study a little harder, and this will translate into long-term success. If the player doesn't want to be successful, then they will sit on the bench and fail.

THE LAST SERVE

I recently heard a story that helped me feel good about the type of life I am attempting to live, and I am sure it is one that Mike will relate highly to as well. It's a story about how the U.S. Navy Seals become Navy Seals, one of the highest performing organizations on the planet. Who makes it through? Who doesn't? The star athletes who have never been truly tested, the premium leaders who are used to delegating to others, and the big tough guys ready to prove their dominance don't make it. The ones who make it are the ones who, when pushed to the absolute brink of emotional and physical exhaustion, dig down deep inside of themselves to find the energy to help the person next to them. Service – giving to others, having their back – is what makes them the highest performing team in the world. It's their willingness to be there for each other.

Mike agrees: As a coach my absolute favorite players are the "junkyard dogs." You never see the junkyard dog spend 30 minutes in the locker room mirror primping. The junkyard dog is the competitor who doesn't care how they look; they just want to help the team. They just want to get after it. They will do whatever it takes to help the team win. The junkyard dog is the first player to help a teammate off the ground. They run to a teammate's defense. They just get things done and they don't hang around after the game looking for accolades and congratulatory statements.

Jay continues: If you've gotten this far into our conversation, then you've likely enjoyed the banter and hopefully learned a few things about the psychology of sports, the art of coaching, and the important life skill development opportunities that surround us all every day. Thank you for reading, and as much as Mike and

I both expressed who we are in the previous chapters, we wanted to leave you with one last declaration here to sum up the life motivation we hold.

Jay takes his shot: *"I love assisting people of the world in creating their ultimate potential."*

Ok Mike's turn! *"It is never about me, it's about them, which is the cowboy way."*

In memory of Jay's tennis dudes:
Kyle, Dan, Ryan, Jerry, Ethan and Drew...

You will all always be an inspiration to me.

MEET THE AUTHORS

Jay M. Harris, MA,
Sport Psychology and Sport Organization

Jay, a native of Lexington, Ohio, was the Head Men's Tennis Coach at Brown University for eight years prior to moving to New York, in 2010, to join the Sportime/John McEnroe Tennis Academy Team. He was the most successful tennis coach in the Brown tennis program's 100-plus year history, leading the team to its highest ever national ranking, #33, two Ivy League Titles, and seven consecutive NCAA Tournament appearances. In 2005, Jay was named the Northeast Region coach of the Year and was a finalist for the National Coach of the Year Award. He coached five singles players and 15 doubles teams to national rankings, including one team that achieved All-American status and two who collectively earned wins over Novak Djokovic, Rafael Nadal and Roger Federer. Prior to Brown, Jay coached at Bowling Green State University where he was named the 2002 Mid-American Conference Coach of the Year after leading the team to MAC Titles in 2000 and 2002. Jay was a successful collegiate player at the University of Cincinnati, graduating with a Bachelor's degree in Psychology. He then earned his Master's degree in Sport Psychology and Sport Organization from Miami University, where he also served as an assistant coach for the women's team winning a MAC title in 1996. In 2024, Jay finished the year ranked #1 in the country in the Men's 50s Doubles USTA rankings.

Michael D. Kathrein, MA,
PGA Associate

Michael holds multiple degrees. He earned his BA in History from The Ohio State University in 1994. He then earned his teaching degree from Ohio Dominican University (1997), and his MA in American History and Government from Ashland University (2010). In 2010, he was selected to represent Ohio at the Presidential Academy by Teaching American History. Michael has taught and coached, in Ohio, at the high school level for 28 years. He has coached boys' and girls' basketball, boys' and girls' golf, baseball, and tennis. As a high school golf coach, Michael has been named Coach of the Year multiple times and has coached at the State Golf Tournament five times. In 2025, Michael was honored with a Distinguished Service Award for his contributions in junior golf. After retiring from high school coaching, he became a PGA Associate. He and his wife Audrey have been married for 27 years and have a daughter, Lainey. Michael's daughter earned her degree from Ashland University and is also a PGA Associate. Michael has combined his extensive education with his vast experience as a player, parent, and coach, to formulate great insights on athletics. Michael's favorite pastime is to walk the golf course and watch Lainey play.

To contact the authors for more information or to book for speaking engagements:

Jay Harris   Harristennisacademy@yahoo.com
Michael Kathrein   Michaelkathrein52@gmail.com

www.ingramcontent.com/pod-product-compliance
Lightning Source LLC
Chambersburg PA
CBHW070133080526
44586CB00015B/1676